Books by Kirby Sommers

Non-Fiction

New! Creating Epstein: Bill Barr, Leslie
Wexner & the CIA
Jeffrey Epstein: Predator, Spy
Jeffrey Epstein, Unsealed (co-written with
Bob Fitrakis)
Bonnie's Clyde: The True Story of Jeffrey
Epstein & Ghislaine Maxwell
Ghislaine Maxwell: An Unauthorized
Biography

Ask Me Anything: About Jeffrey Epstein &
Ghislaine Maxwell (with Bob Fitrakis)
Best of Epstein Project
Epstein Project: Book One
Epstein Project: Book Two
Jeffrey Epstein & El Chapo
Franklin Scandal & Presidio Child Abuse
Power, Money, Politics & Sex

Memoir

The Billionaire's Woman: A Memoir
Cinderella Doesn't Live Here Anymore
Love in the Time of Sickness

Renting in New York

Guerrilla Guide to Renting in NYC
Landlord Links Series

Upcoming Books

Ghislaine Maxwell, Blackmail
Cinderella Doesn't Live Here Anymore

For book giveaways, previews, *Epstein Project* reveals and more:

https://kirbysommers.com/mailing-list

Kirby is also on Twitter:
@kirbysommers

Kirby Sommers

the billionaire's woman

memoir of a sex-slave

Second Edition, 2022

Kirby Sommers

The Billionaire's Woman: Memoir of a Sex Slave

"Never give up. Ever."
-Kirby Sommers

The Billionaire's Woman: Memoir of a Sex Slave

Author's Note

When I was a child I was fascinated by Humpty Dumpty. My mother decorated the bedroom my younger sister and I shared with assorted fairy tales. The requisite twin beds were centered and had enough of a gap that at night, as we shared secrets and giggled, we could reach out and touch each other's fingertips. School books, notebooks and dolls were strewn about the room. The linoleum carpet, chosen for its resiliency by all the mothers in our neighborhood, obscured the hardwood floors. On the shiny surface lived Cinderella, Sleeping

Beauty and the egg-shaped Humpty Dumpty. Before drifting off to sleep, I'd stare long and hard at his two forms. One whole with the other shattered. I pondered all sorts of things. Mainly, I wanted to know what made him fall in the first place. And then, of course, why couldn't he be put back together?

> *"Humpty Dumpty sat on a wall,*
> *Humpty Dumpty had a great fall.*
> *All the king's horses and all the king's men*
> *Couldn't put Humpty together again."*

Even as a six-year-old I was aware that if Humpty Dumpty were to be fixed with bubble gum or the strongest glue, it would be impossible to hide the patching. Lost in these wanderings of my child mind, I'd drift off to sleep.

~

I have written and re-written this book about the most difficult years of my life numerous times. In many ways it has probably been my therapy and saved my sanity. Instead of sitting in a therapist's office with a ticking clock, I worked out the details of a series of events that were out of my control, in written form. The assorted manuscripts that piled up, and which I kept at the bottom of a trunk, never felt complete. They probably would have stayed there because in my mind who really cared if I had been anyone's sex slave? But then two things happened. The *#metoo* movement which blew up after Harvey Weinstein was exposed as a serial rapist. And, the second arrest of Jeffrey Epstein who ran a child sex trafficking ring on July 6, 2019.

The original manuscript of my memoir was written as a work of fiction in 1995—two years after I walked away from Ira Riklis. Since then I have grappled with it—adding scenes, deleting scenes. Leaping forward in time. Going back. It has been my Moby Dick. My quest to catch and control the giant white whale that has evaded me for decades. Each time I usually begin with a current event that somehow triggers me and work backwards. In 2012 that event was the Eliot Spitzer call-girl scandal with Ashley Alexandra Dupré. It is that 2012 manuscript, with minor revisions and added scenes, that I have selected to tell my story. Finally.

PROLOGUE

1986

What happens when a billionaire with the mind of a sex-starved teenage boy and no personal restraints sets his sights on one woman? Under normal circumstances the answer would be marriage. But what if the billionaire is already married and is a closet sex freak?

The kind of freak who has a tissue box at the ready whenever a new issue of Victoria's Secret arrives in the mail, has a stash of girlie magazines neatly stacked away in his safe. A safe that is like a Matryoshka doll—as it is hidden inside a walk-in closet in his office—and indulges in prostitutes-a-la-Spitzer.

A pathetic loser? Some might say.

Think again. It's Ira Riklis, 57-year-old mega rich son of corporate raider and junk bond king Meshulam Riklis. Riklis is also a long-time friend and political contributor to Vice President Joe Biden, Secretary of State Hillary Clinton, Pennsylvania Governor Ed Rendell, former President Bill Clinton and disgraced New York Governor Eliot Spitzer, to name just a very few. And, if birds of a feather ever flocked, then the last two names on this short list proves they do.

Eliot Spitzer

The Eliot Spitzer sex scandal, more than any of the ones preceding or following it, and those yet to be revealed, exposed the fact that men lie about sex and how they get it. Spitzer's sex scandal was brought to light by a government owned software—that among its many functions was used to track money laundering. The official story, though, is that North Fork Bank reported suspicious activity on behalf of Spitzer to the Treasury Department's Financial Crimes Enforcement Network.

As a result, Spitzer had been under surveillance for a period of two years. The place of his downfall was the historic Mayflower Hotel in Washington D.C. The hotel has a sordid past and is known to have been the first place where FBI Director J. Edgar Hoover—a closeted homosexual blackmailed by organized crime with deep ties to Meyer Lansky—enjoyed his first sexual romp with Clyde Tolson. It was at the Mayflower Hotel on February 13, 2008 where Spitzer was caught with a 22-year-old escort named "Kristin". She was later identified as Ashley Dupre. Dupre was one of 50 beautiful young women working for the Emperor's Club—a high-class call-girl ring who sent escorts to New York, Paris, London, Miami and Washington. Spitzer—then Governor of New York had been arranging dates though them on a regular basis using the pseudonym "George Fox".

No one in the sex trade, on either side of the transaction, uses their real name. Or at least very few do. Men who stand on the pinnacle of power and know no harm will ever come to them will use their real name. Spitzer was not among these. His alias George Fox turned out to be the very real name of one of his friends. Jim Cramer in his 2002 book *You Got Screwed* referred to Fox as "Titan Advisors fund-of-funds chief".

Someone was out to nail Eliot Spitzer.

FBI agents were assigned to keep track of the Governor of New York. By listening in on wiretapped conversations, the feds were alerted to an earlier date he'd scheduled for January 26, with the Emperor's Club.

The cloak and dagger spying provided some details. He planned on meeting an escort during the time he was in Washington, D.C. attending a black-tie dinner. The feds had a surveillance team inside the Mayflower Hotel before he even checked in. Spitzer spent a portion of the day and the night at the hotel. But the federal agents left empty-handed. Even though one of them was in a room across the hall from where he maintained a watchful eye through a partially opened door. If Spitzer spent time with a prostitute—she went unnoticed.

As I stated earlier, most "Johns" use fake names. Clearly it was easier for Spitzer to remember a friend's name when paying for sex. Later, in court documents, the names of ten men who were caught were anonymized to numbers. Spitzer became Client 9. The government never named the other men, but they disclosed precise and humiliating details about Spitzer's indiscretions.

Among these, that he'd had seven visits with prostitutes over a period of six months; that he'd spent as much as $80,000 on his habit during the seven years prior to his arrest; that he wanted sex without a condom; and that he kept his black socks on during sex. The latter becoming a running joke in power circles and among those of us who knew what it was like on the inside.

I'd heard about Spitzer's call-girl sex scandal just like everyone else when it became front page news in New York on March 10, 2008. At the time, I was still trying to unravel the mysteries of my life. And, had yet to understand what happens on a personal and political level to someone who crosses the line with a well-connected (and protected) person. In hindsight, when examining the Spitzer scandal, it is clear to see how the power-class looks after their own, and how vicious they become when seeking retribution.

Eliot Spitzer: Sheriff of Wall Street

The FBI took down the Governor of New York on behalf of the power merchants who pull the strings—including their own. While this predator class is not known as oligarchs in the United States—they ought to be. The definition of an "oligarch" is one of few holding power. Among these are the Riklis's and the men in their circle. Men like Maurice "Hank" Greenberg of American International Group (AIG)—known to have begun as a covert CIA operation and presented to the public as an insurance company. It is now one of the largest public companies in the world. One of Ira's sisters, Marica, sat on AIG's Board of Directors for years. Bottom line, Eliot Spitzer broke one the covenant's rules. The super-grifters, who transfer the wealth of a population into their pockets using deceptive practices, will spit you out into the wilderness if you out their secrets to us mere mortals.

~

In 1998 Eliot Spitzer became the Attorney General of New York and held that position for two terms. During that time he earned the nickname "Sheriff of Wall Street". Previous attorney generals in the city stuck to the mandate: consumer fraud. Local level fraud that didn't involve these masters of the universe. They went after crooked auto-repair shops, investigated wrongdoings in nursing homes and chased crooked landlords. Rarely, however, was anything really accomplished even on that level.

Spitzer saw Wall Street as being the largest consumer scam ever perpetuated against the populace in the history of mankind. Using a team of 10 attorneys, he became an enforcer of financial laws. The responsibility really belonged to the Securities and Exchange Commission (SEC)—but they weren't chasing the bad guys. Bernie Madoff is a prime example of how the SEC allows a member of the protected class to steal $50,000,000,000 for two decades and sees nothing.

That is why Eliot Spitzer, the crusader, was knocked off his pedestal in the most embarrassing way possible.

What sticks out in my mind about the scandal is silly. Spitzer didn't take off his black socks while having sex with some of the women. All I could envision was a naked man wearing black socks and so he became, to most people, a cartoon figure to be mocked. I recall it was Roger Stone who made sure everyone digested this morsel. Other details were dropped with gusto by mainstream media and, as the secret life of the once revered governor was exposed, the world went wild. At least it did in New York City and in Washington D.C.

Let's face it. Men cheat. I should be politically correct and say "a lot of men cheat". Few don't. If you're among the short list of women with such a man, hold on to him because he's an anomaly. Spitzer isn't an exception. He is basically the rule.

The monogamous man has been on the list of soon to be extinct mammals for as long as prostitution has existed. It hasn't been labeled the world's oldest profession without the continuously growing demand for the services of the women and men who make this their daily work.

There was a time when I'd ask: "who doesn't know this?" Who doesn't know men cheat? Apparently, a lot of women don't know, or at least they pretend not to.

Before I became jaded, corrupted by things I'd seen, by the life I was forced into, I was extremely naïve and believed, like millions of women around the globe, that only a few married men cheated.

The Eliot Spitzer scandal created a massive sonic meltdown in the hearts of women everywhere. If he cheated on his wife, Silda, the woman who stood by his side silently, bravely, stoically even, as he made his public and televised mea culpa. Silda, the woman who, before our very eyes, aged a decade in a matter of days. Silda, the woman known for her beauty, charm and intelligence. If her husband cheated on her—what did this mean for everyone else? That moment made women everywhere take a sideways glance at their mates and sent many scurrying off to plastic surgeons and anyone peddling botox.

However, what most women of previous generations, my own included, don't realize is there's a huge difference in the way men and women perceive cheating. When a man pays for sex, in his mind, he isn't cheating. I know this first hand. I know this from being told by my clients that seeing me prevented them from cheating. After all, they'd argue: "We're not having an affair. An affair, now, *that* would be cheating."

It was confusing. I'm a woman and to me cheating is cheating. There are no blurry lines. No gray zones. It's definitely black or white.

~

Ira Riklis | Donald Trump

Ira Riklis is the principal of Sutherland Capital Management, Inc., a private holding company primarily involved in the home-security market. The foray into "security" happened after he found me—before venturing into this business Ira explained he ran a private hedge fund company named Sutherland after his sailboat. The company stationary Ira used had a boat design. He also owned a lot of subsidiaries. Even I became a one of these holding companies in time. His firm co-existed with his father's mega conglomerate Rapid American Corporation. They rented a couple of floors in Donald Trump's Fifth Avenue skyscraper— Trump Tower—which at the time was the tallest glass building in Manhattan.

Many shady Russians and others whose ancestors emigrated to the U.S. from Russia, like the Riklis's, had offices or apartments at Trump Tower. It was considered a safe place. A "Cosa Nostra" sort of thing. Trump's building was constructed next door to the world-renowned Tiffany's on Fifty-Seventh Street. In order to build the sort of high rise he wanted Trump purchased the air rights from Tiffany's owner, Walter Hoving, for $5 million. The proximity to Tiffany's made it respectable instead of the sinister and peculiar building it later became.

When the elder Riklis reneged on his lease and stopped paying rent for his luxurious suite of offices and for his apartment (which he shared with his second wife, the pint-sized actress Pia Zadora), sneaking off, as Trump is proud of telling everyone "in the middle of the night" – he sued Riklis for arrears owed and won.

Meshulam Riklis moved out of New York City with his forever young child bride and into the 12-acre estate in Beverly Hills known as Pickfair.

Pickfair had been home to Douglas Fairbanks and Mary Pickford—Hollywood's first power couple. Fairbanks starred in the first movie version of *The Mark of Zorro*. Their home became one of the most celebrated estates in the world – rumored to be "only slightly less important than the White House but much more fun."

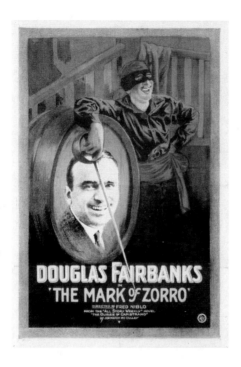

Ira, his son, and the man who forever changed my life stayed in New York City in a new office on East 57th Street, right off Madison Avenue. A portfolio company he owns which is a company he delved into as a direct result of having me hunted down, C.O.P.S. Monitoring, has become the largest wholesale home monitoring company in the world. Combined with sister company, SafeGuard Security (an alarm installation, service and monitoring company), the recurring monthly revenue ranks in the top 50 companies (out of 15,000 companies)

in the United States. In addition to home monitoring he's also involved in commercial "security" accounts.

Other investments include SNIP, a telephone and internet service provider (which I honestly believe he uses even today as a vehicle to spy on me), a hedge-fund consolidation company, a ladies-clothing designer and marketer, a ski-equipment rental chain, various real estate partnerships with an emphasis on strip-shopping centers.

He is also the Vice-Chairman (at least he was when I met him) of Rapid American Corporation—a business that left companies bankrupt and people destitute—with ties to the Mafia (also known as Cosa Nostra which originated in Sicily during the mid-19th century), and notorious gangsters such as Bugsy Siegal and Meyer Lansky (the Jewish Mafia).

Some 20 plus years ago I was the woman Ira Riklis preyed upon, spied on, and coerced into becoming his sex slave. He did this to me at a time in my life when I was the most vulnerable. And he knew it. That is how predators find their victims. They peer into your soul and find the holes. They fool you into believing they can fill those aching gaps for you. They seek out women who have been sexually abused as children, had absent fathers or who are going through periods of low self-esteem. In my case, all three factors were present. If I had been an apple, I would have been the ripest apple on the tree.

Later when I left that world of sex for pay behind and was followed into my real life by can't take no for an answer Ira Riklis who forked over $150,000 to a man named Dave, a former police chief, and instructed him to scour the city of New York in search of a woman whose name he never really knew and who, in fact, never truly existed. Only later, much later when I became his reluctant mistress—scratch that—when he manipulated me into becoming his sex slave, only then did I understand how different cheating was. For men.

Many years after being caught and thrown into the gilded cage that was more like a rotting dungeon, I would be confronted by my own wounded Silda Spitzer in the form of Mrs. Ira Riklis. Except in my case, as I already said, it was really cheating. For a long time.

Years flew by and disappeared down the toilet along with Ira's sperm-filled condoms, which he always insisted I dispose of in the toilet and not in the trash. I never figured out why until the Ira years were over.

The cheating part was confusing at first. Ira was definitely cheating. He is the married one, and the one who lies to his wife, as well as everyone around him daily. But was I cheating? Was I complicit? I knew I had to lie to protect him, and I did. I lied and protected him even after I didn't have to lie anymore.

24

Every now and again my thoughts would stray to Patty Hearst, the granddaughter of William Randolph Hearst who in 1974 was kidnapped by the Symbionese Liberation Army (SLA). She was raped and threatened with death. The image of her cradling an M1 carbine rifle and robbing a bank haunted me for a long time. I knew she been brainwashed by her captors—it was her sensational abduction and subsequent crimes that made the words "Stockholm Syndrome" part of the American vernacular.

Stockholm Syndrome is described as a condition in which a hostage develops a psychological bond during the intimate time spent with his or her captor. And while I didn't fully understand what that meant regarding my life in general and my years with Ira, I sometimes felt a symbiotic bond with Hearst. There wasn't a lot of difference between what happened to her and what happened to me. The image of her walking willingly into a bank with a weapon to rob it and the image of me walking willingly into a bedroom with Ira seemed similar. I didn't know freewill for a long time. I protected my abuser, the man who used my body as a trash receptacle for his sperm with no regard for my well-being—I protected him for many years even after I found the courage to break free.

ONE

_____

"Once in, never out." The Johnny Carson look alike with a cigarette the size of a small brown stump dangling on his lip looking like it was about to pop out and hit me in the eye is giving me the once and the twice over. I am now officially merchandise and it doesn't feel good at all.

I try not to fidget as I stand in what looks like someone's apartment, in a living room where the furniture is still new and unused. Except this isn't anyone's home. It's a bordello on Fifth Avenue in New York City, and it's similar to hundreds of other make-believe apartments neatly tucked away across Manhattan where women sell themselves to businessmen every day from 9 to 5, and where neighbors never suspect anything of this sort is happening.

My heart is going thumpety, thump, thump. It's almost lodged in my throat. My palms are clammy and I wonder if I'm going to make it through the interview. I tentatively lift my eyes up from where they're glued to his brown penny loafers and dare look at him. He's wearing a preppy sweater vest under a white shirt with khaki pants. Geez, who knew pimps looked like someone's dad?

I was raped, lost my job as administrative assistant, and my floundering new business as a fashion designer was suddenly in the toilet. So much for going at it on your own. I am standing here in four-inch stilettos with a short pink dress I wore to a friend's wedding. My belly is only slightly swollen and doesn't betray my missed period and confirmed pregnancy. When I asked my ex-boyfriend for help by explaining I'd been raped he didn't believe me. After living with him for five years I'd left him only a couple of months before renting a one-bedroom apartment a little over 10 blocks away from our place. He was still upset that I'd left and even more upset that *his* "little girl"— as he liked referring to me—had sex with another man.

And so, he wasn't listening or caring or just wanted revenge when I tried to explain how it happened. My movie date wrestled my keys away from me as I tried opening the front door to the building I just moved into, shoved me into the elevator like I was his prisoner, and once it stopped on my floor, he ushered me out demanding I tell him which one of the many keys to use, threatening to slice my face. Once inside, he dragged me by the hair and pushed me up against the wall. I tried to fight him off, but with one fist he knocked me off my feet, and onto to the floor. My head bounced off the wall and suddenly the thought that I might die rushed into my mind. Before I could scream, he was on top of me and I couldn't breathe. I'd read somewhere that if you do nothing, don't fight back, you won't die. My mind was racing with a hundred thoughts and all of them were about surviving this moment. And so, I didn't fight back and in I don't know how many minutes it was over. I felt powerless as I lay there, half dressed, broken and in pain. I glanced at his face which was void of expression except for a sinister smirk, and watched as he pulled up his pants, which he hadn't taken off, buckled his belt and left.

The term "date-raped" had yet to be invented in the world of mergers and acquisitions, fast money and neon-lit Studio 54 of 1980s New York. What kind of girl gets raped, unless I really wanted it? That had been my ex's take on it and there was no way he was going to help me with the $200 I needed to get an abortion. As uncomfortable as it felt to stand in front of Johnny Carson's double, it's even more frightening to think about having the baby. Would I be just like my mother? No way was I going to risk that.

His words began to bounce back and forth in my mind: *"Once in, never out."* Not for me, I chanted quietly. Not for me. Not for me. I'll get out. Not for me.

"How old are you anyway? I don't sell kids."

"Old enough," I retorted in an out of body kind of half hallucinatory state. This could not really be happening to me. I was practically a virgin. I knew the names and the dates of the guys I had slept with. I could count them on one hand. I mentally renamed myself the virgin whore.

"Take your clothes off. Let me see what you look like." Warren's voice was huskier now and I didn't like how this was going at all. My eyes immediately darted to my older sister's face and sensing my fear she flashed him a cold look shaking her head.

It felt protective and I was grateful. In that moment, I forgot I had gone to her to borrow the $200 my ex had denied me. Instead she talked me into coming here so I could, in her words "earn the money".

Getting raped, finding out I was pregnant and then discovering my older sister knew people like this was more than I could handle. I didn't understand the betrayal until many years later because for maybe twenty years I was in a state of shock.

I'll never really know why she decided to sell me to a pimp and in all the many years since I've never asked her. Perhaps it was her way of getting even with the infant my mother saddled her with when she was only just 14-years-old. Or, maybe it's because the bad blood that has existed between my mother and myself had been passed on to her where, like thick black tar, it's sealed off every pore of my skin.

I am painfully reminded of being alone in the world as I hear the Johnny Carson look alike speak and feel his eyes on me. I would spend the rest of my life trying to cleanse myself of the stain her actions and this moment placed on my body and on my soul.

It was the beginning of a long dark and hellish journey and if I could slip back into time, I would march right back to that day, to that moment, and bolt for the door leaving them in their make-believe world of sex-for-pay in a fake apartment.

I am lulled back by his insisting tone.

"You have a beautiful sister, Gigi, why deny me the pleasure of seeing the goods?"

Whatever small part of me which held out hope that someone, anyone—my ex-boyfriend, my mother, my sisters, a stranger on a white horse, would somehow rescue me, have faded.

Two

The rules: never show up at the Fifth Avenue apartment building wearing anything remotely sexy. Wear jeans and look like a college kid or the neighbors might get wise. Bring your call girl paraphernalia and the clothes you're going to wear in a duffle bag. Do not wear them on the street or you could be followed to the apartment.

Always get the money up front. Never talk about the money. Don't use the word *money*. Remind him to leave the money *there* which means the nightstand next to the bed, *only* tell him after he's taken off everything. Everything means his socks, too. If he keeps his socks on, he's not naked. If he refuses to get naked tell him he's got to leave. If he's naked and he's a cop, he can't arrest you. Never touch the money. Don't count the money. Scoop up the cash from the night stand after he's naked and gotten "comfortable" which means he's lying on the bed. Close the bedroom door before handing the money to Warren in the office. Always give Warren the money before beginning the session. At the end of the day you get 50% of what you make. Everyone takes turns. First to arrive gets first dibs. Unless you have repeat business. Always wear lingerie. Always wear a skirt or a dress. Never wear your lingerie to the door with nothing over it when answering the door. If you do, he's going to turn into a "looky-loo" leave and go jerk off by himself. You don't get paid when he jerks off by himself. Never wear pants. A woman in pants doesn't excite men unless it's a special request. Never bring up his wife. Keep current on the news so you can keep up your end of the conversation. Never hog the conversation. Learn to listen. Men like to talk. Never use your real first name and again don't blab about your personal life. This comes handy in the event you run into a stalker. Never be the one to insist on using a condom. Nothing is more terrifying to a penis than wrapping it in a baggie. You don't follow these rules, you're out, there are 50 other girls who will take your place. Remember, you girls are as disposable as the tissue I use to sneeze into.

~

I'm a wild mess on the morning that divides my life into before and after. It's only a little past 8 a.m. and I'm scheduled to get there at 10:45 a.m. I've been playing records to help me calm down. *'Beast of Burden'* by the Rolling Stones is sending its vibes into my livingroom and so I get up and start dancing. I try to remember what my sister explained about giving a blow-job. She taught me with a banana, but really, I don't know if I learned anything. I've done that but for like a second with my ex. I don't know if I can do that for a stranger.

I belt out Mick Jagger's words and do my best imitation of his swag.

> *I'll never be your beast of burden*
> *My back is broad but it's a hurting*
> *All I want is for you to make love to me*

Gigi, my older sister, who has hated me since I was a kid and who has taken me to this threshold instructed me to make believe I was making love with my boyfriend. She was like my second mom and I always tried to make her like me. The three of us sisters look different. For many years Gigi has had short cropped hair she dyed a strawberry red. I never understood why she wants to look like a boy when all she does is try to get the attention of men.

Oh, little sister
Pretty, pretty, pretty, pretty, pretty girls
Uh you're a pretty, pretty, pretty, pretty, pretty, pretty
girl
Pretty, pretty, such a pretty, pretty, pretty girl
Come on baby please, please, please

The money I've scoured my apartment for is laid out on my miniature dining table. There are two single dollar bills and a smattering of coins. As I move my hips in sync with the music it's difficult not to focus on the $4.87 sitting next to my forgotten breakfast. My dry bowl of cornflakes cereal and Cuban coffee, which is really the only thing I know how to make, is untouched. I can't eat. I have enough money to take the bus there, get back and get a slice of pizza afterwards.

I suddenly remember I don't know what I'm going to wear to be a call-girl so I turn off my record player, put the album back in its cover, and run into my bedroom.

Pushing open the sliding door of my closet my bed quickly becomes a collage of discarded clothes as I frantically scrutinize outfit after outfit. On. Off. On. Off. I shuffle back and forth to the narrow full-length mirror I got at the five and dime. I was able to glue it to the front of the bathroom door and can see all of me. I slip into the four-inch heels I've placed in the hallway just in front of the mirror and before examining the latest outfit I place my hands over my swollen belly. Bowing my head, I talk to my baby.

"I'm really sorry. It would be irresponsible for me to have you. I'm very sorry. Truly I am. What happens if I'm like your grandmother? Trust me, you don't want to relive my childhood. I can't let that happen to you. And I can't become her, please understand. Forgive me, okay?"

THREE

I am a child of divorced parents. I have two sisters who look nothing like me. We're so different all I do almost every day of my childhood is to wonder if I am adopted. My daydreams are full of fantasies that often take the form of having my mother take the wrong baby home by mistake.

My real mother, the one I yearn for, the one that resembles the mothers on TV, I cling to the hope that one day she'll burst through the front door, reclaim me as her child and hold me close to her where it is safe and warm and loving.

Meanwhile, the mother I'm stuck with who beats me with her fists with hate contorting her face, and who whips me with a belt while she screams, and tells me how horrible I am, until welts cover my body, and who allows her boyfriends and the other men who pay to rent a room in our apartment to touch me in my private places, this mother decides early on that of her three daughters, I am the one most likely to succeed in finding the *'right man'*. A euphemism she uses for rich man. So, she stops short of killing me because I will, someday when I am grown up, I will do right by her and prove to her that I am not the despicable unlovable child she has made me believe I am.

At 14, she figures I don't need an education for this, so I am taken out of school like my older sister was 14 years earlier to help mom with me when I was born. This put an end to my sister's education and would poison her heart against me for the rest of our lives.

Handing me a broom, mom orders me to start sweeping. "One day," her voice is shrill and angry. "You'll marry someone rich and buy me a yellow house." I swear she made me believe I owed her something. And I paid. With my life, with my body, and with every broken shred of my young soul, I paid.

Fortunately, I suffer a mild heart attack. I am in bed for six months, and it is here in my bedroom, with the wall of infirmity keeping her at bay that I discover I can push her world away and disappear into my own. I've been a reader since I was a toddler, and now left alone, I devour my schoolbooks. I lose myself in daydreams. I want to become an archeologist, or an actress, or a writer, or a business tycoon. I begin to feel better and know I'm not meant to stay in this hell sweeping floors.

When her lover, the neighborhood doctor, comes in to examine me, always closing my bedroom door for what he calls "privacy," and unbuttons my pajama top to take a look see at my newly formed breasts cupping them before pressing the cold stethoscope against my skin, I know it is the only chance I'll have.

I'm frozen and terrified as I feel his hand cup my right breast and try to avert his unblinking stare that is waiting for get a response from me. I can feel his breath on me. I stare right back. Almost defiantly.

My words come out slowly. "Mommy... doesn't... want me... to... go back to... school. Please... talk her... out... of... it. I want to go back... please..." At 70, he still has a full head of hair. It's the color of snow. His clear blue eyes and wide grin don't disguise the fact that he's a dirty old man. From the time I was teeny he's been part of mom's life. He's a Zionist and he's taught me about the holocaust and how he and his family made it out of Russia only to find themselves victims of the Nazi's. I've spent many afternoons learning how to type in his office, drafting letters for his patients, and I've seen up close the dark tattoo numbers on all of their arms. What a crazy world this is. Some of them are even drug addicts. They're all suffering from different illnesses and despite the fact they all look to him as if he's a god, he's always frightened me.

I used to believe my mother was in love with him. I didn't know she was using him as she would use me in years to come. But that day, when the dirty old guy was busy feeling me up in my bedroom, I got lucky. He must have said something to my mother, because after that day I was allowed to go back to school.

I am even given the opportunity of skipping a grade because the months spent studying in bed have gotten me past 11th grade requirements. But I opt to stay with my class. I am happy to be among my friends, and even more grateful that for a few hours every weekday I am not home with her.

～

"You're just like your father!" My mother's face has that look. I brace myself for another beating - one I know I don't deserve. I'm a good girl. I've proven myself to be a good student. I am even shy. Too shy and withdrawn to look for ways to displease her, but somehow, I always do.

I wonder why my younger sister, who's only one year my junior, is treated differently. Why is she loved and I'm not? The answer waits for me far into the future, when I'm a grown woman and inadvertently learn the truth. My younger sister is my mother's love child, and I indeed am just like my father. I won't know for decades to come that she married him only because she needed a husband to care for her and three children from her first marriage. Her first husband died of tuberculosis when she was only 21 years old.

When I finally learn this truth, I'll realize that I remind her of a marriage to a man she didn't love. I will go back in time and try to make sense of the fact that when she looked at me, she saw him – in the twinkle of my eyes, in the slope of my high cheekbones, in my quest to be creative, in my generous spirit, and in my resilience. However, as much as I fight to be nothing like her, I realize that in her womb, through the DNA she's imprinted on me, like a stamp in a passport, I have inherited her ability and her will to survive too. It is the only trait both my parents share: an incredible ability to endure a great deal of suffering.

FOUR

_____

At 17 I fall in love with more than just the written word. I find magic in blank sheets of paper and in yards of uncut fabric. During this year as I prepare to graduate at the top percentile of my class, I write my first magazine article. To my amazement and delight, it becomes a front cover two-part series.

On the heels of this incredible feat, I win a Beauty Pageant. I am resplendent in my tiara, cradling an armful of roses, the popping flash of cameras surrounding me create an illusion of large colorful balloons and behind the glow of this moving collage I hear a booming voice announce I've won a brand new car, a trip to the Caribbean, a cash prize and dozens of other goodies. It's bewitching and seductive.

The contest had been my mother's idea. She'd paraded me around the series of events for months. I wore hot pants and tank tops and high heels and make-up and teased out my hair and pranced around dirty old men. But for reasons unknown to me she didn't like the dress I'd been able to find on the same day as the finals. I wore it for her. A long white slender gown with slits down the side of my legs. She hated it, called me a whore and told me she wouldn't be caught dead sitting next to me that night.

I couldn't believe it. All the other parents, and for sure the mothers of all the contestants, were going to be there. This was the night. And really, she never let me out of the apartment on my own or with a boyfriend before. I didn't understand how she was going to let me go at all but she did. I left with my 17-year-old high school boyfriend a couple of hours later.

It took a long time for me to realize she'd found a new way to torture me now that I was grown. A more subtle way to hurt me: psychological torment.

The whole blow out with her was almost a blur when the crown was placed on my head and I cradled the flowers in my arms. As I walked down the small stage, I thought to myself *"I can do anything"*. Someone held my hand and walked me off the stage so I could address the crowd of reporters.

The paparazzi were all around me and some of the guards were trying to get them to keep their distance. I tried to find my boyfriend's face in the crowd but I couldn't see anything because of the popping of the cameras. A reporter thrust a microphone close to my face. "Your parents must be very proud of you tonight. Can you point them out to me?" I was stunned by his question and suddenly felt claustrophobic. I pushed past him and through the crowd as the cameras kept flashing and the questions kept coming.

I held on to my tiara which I could feel was lopsided as a ran for shelter into the women's restroom. To my relief there was only one woman inside. She congratulated me and grinned broadly.

I thanked her and asked her for a quarter so I could call my mother. I've got to tell her I won. I'm not worthless mom, I'm not.

Winning changed nothing. For a short while it gave mom something else to brag about and more cash because she took my winnings. It hurt but wasn't too surprising since she had been taking whatever money I earned from the time I began to work at the age of 13.

And even though all I really had was my tiara and my memories, it was still a magical moment even if I didn't get to keep my money. When we went to the car dealership for the photo op I did as she instructed, and told them that I wanted the cash instead. She nixed the Caribbean trip too. For many years, whenever I saw the model of the car I'd won on the streets of New York, it stung like the death of a beloved pet.

If I had to choose between these two memorable events of my 17th year, I would choose the former. Getting published topped the beauty pageant. Seeing my words on the printed page struck a deeper chord inside me.

So, I fend off the offers for a modeling career that begin to pour in and am curiously aware that I don't want to use my looks to get through life, it would be way too easy.

I have come to accept that I am pretty. I also know I want more, and have great belief that I can get it with my other gifts, which aren't as visible. Except that even as I tell myself this, my hopes for my future are defined by what I see around me, and it is what I do not want to become which frightens me. The ugliness of the neighborhood, the random violence, the bitterness of my mother; and I realize deep within the soft curve of my belly, deep in this newly emerged woman's body, that somehow my looks are the way out of here. In this reality, how was I to know that Ira Riklis, living in luxury, already married, is beginning to wait for me?

I start to design and sell my own clothing line and I am beginning to get the better of that little voice inside my head that reminds me I am nobody, that I've no idea how to talk to people, that I've no idea what I'm doing standing in a showroom, or in someone's store selling my work, when all I really want to do is run and hide.

Even as this is happening, I know it stems from the abuse which has changed from physical to mental torture by my mother. The panic attacks come on suddenly and I am trying to teach myself out of them. I know I can overcome this.

Just as I taught myself my schoolwork when I was sick, and how I taught myself to sew, I am adamant that I will win, and so I don't run. I face it, and just as I am close enough to touch the light, the unthinkable happens. I am date raped and discover to my horror I'm pregnant.

CHAPTER FIVE

Who knew it'd be so difficult to find something to wear that I'd probably only have on for five minutes? I settle on a cute white dress I made the previous summer. The color symbolizes purity and given my shameful lack of experience it's the perfect choice. I push aside a pile of clothes and lay it flat on the bed, folding it carefully, and then tucking it into my duffle bag next to the stockings and garterbelt GiGi lent me.

Warren gave strict orders to get there early and be 'trick ready' by 11 am. Before dashing out, I search for the small bottle of vodka I know my ex left inside the kitchen somewhere. As soon as I find it crack it open and pour it all down my throat. 'Yuk!" It's sharp and acidy and it stings. I've never drank before but maybe this will help. I slip inside the bathroom and squish squash with Listerine. Pressing myself over the sick I peer closely into the mirror on the medicine chest. My reflection does nothing to betray how I feel. My lips are perfectly lined and only my lipstick needs a touch up. I dig out of my handbag my bright pink lipstick and slick it fast across my lips.

It's a pretty sunny day and doesn't betray the darkness of my fear. I'm greeted by the cacophony of honking horns, barking dogs, jackhammers, the occasional siren, and the never-ending snippets of conversations that make up the urban acoustic orchestra unique only to Manhattan.

A few joggers, nannies pushing baby strollers, and an older couple holding hands walk past me as I march across the street towards the bus stop. I wonder if anyone of them can see into my duffle bag and know I'm on sale today. I quickly feel my face blush and push the moronic thought out of my mind. The bus arrives and I climb on. Forty-five minutes later it delivers me to my new life.

~

"Have you decided on a new name?" The blonde asks as she piles on another layer of makeup to her already fully made up face.

There's a bleached blonde, a raunchy redhead, a cocoa colored ex Vegas showgirl, and I realize I'm now the obligatory befuddled brunette.

"Page. I'm going to call myself Page." It's the last name of a girl in a book I just read and for the short amount of time I plan to be in the business it'll do.

"Pretty name for a pretty girl. I'm stuck with the crappy name I gave myself."

"What's that?"

"Dixie. Can't change it now, my regulars wouldn't like it." She whines.

Great, I think to myself, I'm talking to a woman who actually gave herself a white trash name.

We're all crammed into the office which is really just a large dining table pushed against the rear of the living room by the windows. Floor to ceiling plush velvet red drapes hang about 6 feet away from the windows hiding and separating it from the rest of the room. A client walking into the place would never guess that behind the dramatic curtains sit about half a dozen people.

There is also the radio. It listens to what's happening in the bedroom in real time. All of us can hear what the client tells the girl and vice versa. Warren explained to me that it's for our protection. He said sometimes a client gets violent and he has to keep an ear open for these sorts of things. In the bedroom the listening device is taped behind the dresser. I will soon learn it's not our safety he's concerned about, it's about making sure his clients and his cash don't walk out the door with any of us.

The office is the hub of the apartment. It's where the phones ring and appointments are scribbled into the daily planner, and where everyone hides whenever a client shows up.

Monastic silence is the rule whenever a "John" arrives at the front door until he is led by whoever is *up* into the bedroom. At which point it's okay to whisper amongst ourselves or poke fun at the sounds coming out of the two-way radio. Whenever a client is in the apartment it always feels to him like it's just him and the girl.

Even though the office has oversized windows overlooking Fifth Avenue and would likely have wonderful rays of sun flowing into the room, there isn't anything to look at and no light gets inside. Instead there is a layer of aluminum foil over which hang a second set of floor length curtains. When I asked about the foil

Warren explained that it keeps the apartment cool. To me, it felt like a prison. Being inside a make-believe apartment with no natural light and no way to see the outside makes one feel like you're living on another planet. Which is exactly where we all were.

"Ladies stop the chatter. You're next, greenhorn." Warren's motioning me up with his thumb.

I still have not been able to figure out how I'm supposed to have sex with a guy I don't even know and somehow the moment is here and there's no turning back. A parallel universe has taken the place of the world as I knew it. Everything that was right is suddenly wrong and upside down. Nothing makes sense, and I begin to float away from the core of the little girl who had stoically overcome all the turbulences thrown her way.

I think about Warren's new name for me Green Horn. The horn of a newly slaughtered animal. He's right. I am already fragmented.

He's very tall and well-built and blond and appears to be only in his late twenties walks in.

"Hell---ooo---O!" he exclaims with a slight accent.

I echo the salutation and robotically usher him into the bedroom. I can't believe someone so young wants to pay for sex. But here he is. And I have to go through with this. The butterflies in my stomach are racing around in full force. From this moment on, I will never be me again or like anyone else I will ever meet.

What was the use of fighting my way back into school and staying up way into the night reading Edith Wharton novels while everyone else was sleeping? Instead of marrying someone for money, like mom always wanted me to, I am about to sell myself for a couple of dollars. It's so deeply embarrassing. I feel the shame spread like a bad rash deep into my soul and over my skin. Does he see it, I wonder? Do I even look the same?

"Wow, you're so gorgeous. I never expected to see such a beautiful woman. Happy boy I am," he's got a really deep and loud voice. They're going to have no trouble hearing him in the office. He sheds his clothes in less than a minute and without my even asking he put the money on the nightstand beside the bed. It's clear to me he has done this before. I'm the newbie. I quickly glance at his left hand searching for a wedding band, but he doesn't have one. And then I wonder for the second time why a good-looking single guy is paying for sex.

"Some men take off their wedding rings, but don't take anything for granted, just don't ask them if they're married or not," was the advice one of the girls gave me, so didn't ask.

His enormous erection was already standing at attention and pointed directly at my white dress.

Plopping himself down on the bed he extends his arm to me.

Ignoring it, I snap up the five crisp twenties and walk out of the room with an exaggerated sway of my hips.

"I'll be right back!"

When I re-enter the bedroom, I find he's already busy stroking himself. He looks at me with the same psychotic eyes Malcolm McDowell had in the film *Clockwork Orange..*

"How do you like this?" He sneers through clenched teeth. His eyelids hang heavy over his eyes that are glued on my body.

The rape comes back to me and I see no difference between this and that.

"…all for you baby. Take everything off. I want you to sit on my face and I want to lick your pussy," his voice is deep and ominous.

I stand very still and for a second think about running. But where will I go? He's paid for me. Slowly, I push off the shoulder straps of my dress and it drops to my waist. His moaning grows louder as I wiggle it past my hips. My pristine white dress lands like a pile of forgotten garbage on the floor.

I step over it as his hand grabs mine. One hand reaches for me and the other is wrapped around his cock, stroking faster and harder.

"Take everything off! I want to see your body!"

I pull my hand away from his and try to get comply.

The stockings were, as expected, already baggy around my knees and so I kick off my high heels, push off the stockings, and snap off the garterbelt tossing them onto my forgotten dress. Before I can unhook my bra, he yanks me onto the bed, lifting me up by the waist where he puts me back down on top of his face.

His tongue flickers inside me while his hands sink into the flesh of my round ass. He moans and I simply echo the sound back to him. This is not like making love to your boyfriend. And then he lifts me again and drops me down on the bed. He spreads my legs open and plunges deep inside of me. His body goes into convulsions and I wonder if he's dying because he's so large he might crush me to death too.

And then, it's over.

He cups my face, pulls me back toward him and whispers into my ear: "How much to stay the day?" I know they're listening and so I am grateful to him in that small moment that he said this quietly into my ear. I place my mouth next to his ear and whisper back, "Sorry, I'm booked."

Six

My life becomes unrecognizable to me. For a long time after my first encounter with a John, I'd wake up every morning with the weight of a deep mournful sorrow you usually feel when someone you truly love has died. For a fraction of a second, I'd forget, and then suddenly it would envelope me and I knew it is my own death I mourned.

No one told me these men would want to spend two or three hours or even a whole day with me. No one told me about the petty jealousy of the other women whose clients clamored to see "the new girl". No one told me that a "regular" is like gold to them and having me as a distraction meant that in addition to having to pretend with a *"John,"* I'd have to survive the hatred of these women. None of it made sense. It was an upside-down world. In real life I was taught women don't show a man how smart they are, and in this world for sex that was considered okay – just don't be prettier than the other women on sale. It was here when I discovered that women would be the first to deceive you. That there was such a thing as female misogyny. It hadn't been just my mother and my sisters. It was an issue for a lot of women. Throughout the rest of my life I remained cautious around other women and found myself trusting men a lot more. Men only lied to get sex. They didn't lie about anything else.

Mara waved me over to the sofa, patting it with her hand so I could sit next to her. She was the nicest of the group of people in the make-believe apartment. Her large duffle bag sat on the floor and she reached, pulled out a photograph and silently handed it to me. It was a tall dazzling Las Vegas showgirl with a perfect figure and a perfect face and a happy smile.

"How beautiful," I exclaimed. "Who is she?"

"Me," Mara giggled. In a hushed tone she said, "I learned how to knock myself down a couple of notches because of the jealousy of the other dancers in Vegas. I still do. And missy-whatever-your-real-name is, you're going to have to learn this too if you want to survive here."

Mara had already told me she had been abandoned by her powerful boyfriend after she gave birth to a deformed baby girl. No doubt a direct result of all the drugs he plied her with was her take on it. He took one look at the baby when she was born, peeled off a couple of hundred-dollar bills, scribbled a phone number on a piece of paper and abandoned her in a Vegas hospital. The number belonged to a madam. Mara was so distraught when she realized she wasn't going to be able to afford the medical bills for her new-born that she made the terrifying phone call. That was nine years ago.

She was the nicest person I'd met during this time of my life and left me with words I carry to this day, "Never cast your pearls to swines". It took me a long time to truly understand the meaning of those words.

I was able to get the abortion two weeks after becoming a human garbage receptacle for the sperm of a series of nameless men. I called a friend and he accompanied me to the clinic. It was a couple of blocks away from the 34th Street Macy's department store. We took the subway there, and as we approached the building, we were accosted by half a dozen protesters filled with rage. They shouted "You murderers!" into our faces. Their anger echoed my own.

I sat alone huddled on my sofa for two weeks sobbing uncontrollably while I tried to heal. The abdominal pain was intense, the loss of blood was so severe that my skin turned ash white, and I could barely walk. When it was time to pick up and resume my life—neither it, nor I, were there.

I'm inextricably, undeniably lost. There's nothing left of me. Whatever strength I possess is gone. I cannot go back to being whomever it was I used to be and find myself slipping further into a life void of reality. "Not for me!" I'd silently protest every morning. Not for me. Not for a girl who is still shy and more than a bit naïve.

Within weeks I find myself retreating into that little place inside of me which has guided me for as long as I can remember, and decide that if I can't go *back*, I certainly won't stay *here* in a low-class house with three other girls. I get my own working apartment and up the fee. To avoid intercourse, I teach myself to strip, I teach myself to listen, and I teach myself to talk to these rich and powerful men. I become the most sought-after call girl in New York City; as well as the most reclusive person on the planet, so much so even my clients can't reach me. One of my regulars who works at the White House told me, "You're more difficult to reach than the President of the United States." And he was right, I was.

However, I am also sexually traumatized. I have been reduced to parts of my body: breasts, vagina, ass, hair, lips. I am stunned at how quickly I learn to fake it. To feign happiness for the gratification of a man's sexual and personal ego. To pretend that what they have to say is all I want to hear. To look into their horny eyes, limp lips, and stiff dicks and pretend to be in love with them. What astounded me just as much was that they appeared to believe it. No matter how fat, how old, or how despicable any of these men were – they truly believed they were special to me.

Except that now Ira Riklis will find me. I exist in a world *he* frequents and I will never be able to escape him. He is my Jack the Ripper. When he finds me he will tear into my young flesh where he will keep his claws in my body, in my soul, for the rest of my life.

≈

I jump out of the yellow cab that stops an inch away from the curb steps from the polished doorway of the building where I have my working apartment. There is no doorman. No one to record the comings and goings of any of the men who are my clientele, and it is for this reason that I chose the clean, but modest looking building to begin with. There is only a double entrance

59

doorway with an intercom that rings into my apartment via the phone.

To my delight there is no one in the lobby. The chrome and mirror elevator doors slide open and I step in alone. The woman in the mirror looks back at me with a confidence I don't necessarily share.

I stare at my reflection and see a mane of dark hair cascading down over shoulders stopping just below my tiny waist and just above my rounded buttocks. Wisps of it tickle my perfectly oval face, which surprisingly, looks unscathed by the extreme change in the circumstances of my life. I see my father's dark slightly slanted eyes, high cheekbones, and full lips, all of which makes me look as if I am partly Oriental and which is possibly the reason men have labeled me exotic.

My lips are lined and glossy and although I am still in my sweats, I know I look good. I know this because every time I walk anywhere eyes follow me, no matter if I dress up or down. But for reasons that remain unclear to me, I do not know the extent of how my beauty affects those around me. Especially men.

During this time in my life I will never remember what I look like unless I am peering into a mirror. The elevator lined with mirrors stops quietly on my floor and I immediately stop scrutinizing the face of the girl looking back at me. I have been absent from me for a long time.

My day is booked and I would have loved to stay home because I woke up feeling like I'm PMSing and I'm irritable. With bills to pay I push myself into the day. There are days and weeks on end that I cannot bring myself to stepping foot into my work apartment. On the days I do work, like today, I am always booked and always know in advance who I am going to see and what I am going to wear with every one of my clients.

My clientele are regulars. I know what they like. There are no surprises and they're well aware that if they do not book their appointment in advance, chances of seeing me are as slim as spotting a unicorn crossing the street.

Scooping up copies of The Wall Street Journal piled by the door I hear the phone ringing softly behind it. I quickly unlock the door and walk into the modestly furnished apartment I use for my upscale clients, tossing the newspapers on the sofa so I could catch up on my reading. Tidbits about most of my clients show up regularly in most of the financial newspapers and magazines. Staying in the loop about who was doing what always came in handy when pillow talk inevitably turns to business talk.

The red blinking light of my answering machine catches my eye but I don't have a chance to listen to my messages before the phone begins to ring once again. It's only 10am and my first appointment with a well-known actor isn't until 11:30 but it might be him and so I reach for the receiver.

"Hi," says an unfamiliar voice.

"Hi," I parrot back, waiting for him to say something else so I could recognize his voice like I do with everyone I know.

"I was hoping I'd have a chance to meet you today. My name is Ira." The tone in his voice tells me he is elegant and overly confident. But I am not familiar with him and then I realize he is new and suddenly wish I hadn't answered at all.

I don't need a new client. I have enough to keep me busy and safe. In any event I'm not even in a good mood so I say nothing and stall as I try to figure out how I am going to rid myself of him.

"I'm sorry Ira, I no longer make new friends."

For 30 seconds there is only silence and I wonder if he hung up.

"I'll make it worth your while," the voice returns in a less aggressive manner but still persistent. I can already tell he is not someone accustomed to the word "no".

"I don't know Ira, I really don't make new…"

"How about I double your going rate?" He interrupts me mid-sentence.

"Well…Ira, I don't like making a deal with anyone I don't know," and then I stop and ask: Ira *what…* exactly?"

My left hand automatically reaches for my appointment book along with a pen. I'm jostling the receiver between my shoulder and my chin as I flip the pages open while mulling over the possibility of maybe finding an open spot for him.

"Ira what?" I repeat as I write him name with a large question mark on the margin of the page.

"Just Ira," he replies.

And because he didn't give me a last name, even a fake last name, I know he is legit. He isn't a cop. He only wants what they all want I conclude.

I then shift gears because an appointment doesn't begin when the guy is in the apartment. The appointment, as far as I am concerned, begins at hello. I lower my voice a notch and slow down my words

"What time are you thinking of?"

"Now would be good."

I let out a couple of giggles. Soft child-like giggles that are both real and not. I mean, they're my real giggles, but I didn't particularly want to giggle other than to make him feel like what he said was amusing. Making the client feel comfortable is always your number one thing. Making them come is secondary.

Because when a man is comfortable, he always achieves his orgasms.

"Now, let's not be greedy. How about one o'clock? Is that okay?"

"If it's not okay, I'll make it okay."

I felt his sense of victory over the line and went into my appointment book scribbling his name next to the one o'clock slot.

What a lucky beast I think to myself since my one o'clock appointment called me yesterday to reschedule.

Time always disappears in this apartment and before I have a chance to catch up on my reading it's almost time for my 11:30. I never think of their names I only remember their time slot. 11:30, 1pm, 3pm. It never occurs to me that perhaps I am too am the same for them: a phantom of sorts.

Wellesley, a famous Hollywood actor, and therefore not his real name, arrives fifteen minutes late making me stress out about the new guy, Ira, and his time slot. Wells walks in with a bit of a stagger and I know he's high on something.

Geez, I think to myself, this is not going to be pleasant.

"Hi honey, are you okay?" I wrap my arm around his waist and walk him straight toward the bed.

"Yeah, yeah, I'm okay. Just having a hard time getting into the day, that's all. Nothing for you to worry about." His deep raspy voice is reassuring. He sinks heavily into the bed and pulls off a cowboy boot, then throws it clear across the room with a heave. More than anything I don't want him to die in my apartment.

I kneel down and begin to pull the other one off because other than the possibility of him having a heart attack and keeling over I do not want him to scruff up my freshly painted walls.

"Ahh, sweetheart you don't have to do that," he tries to pull his foot away from me but I keep a grip on it.

"It's okay Wells. Just sit back and relax."

He acquiesces and I manage to pull off his boot and then peel off his socks. And while I am helping him undress, I can't help but to think about how sad his life appears. At the height of his career he was quite the guy and had girlfriends like Natalie Wood and other beautiful glamour girls.

Now, he just seems like a beat-up old druggie who pops valiums like candy, chasing them with liquor. He has nothing left but his memories and the little bit of money he was able to keep from spending on drugs and women that he plans to use to resurrect his career. Except that he's always somewhat sedated – and I can't tell whether it's drugs or a physical illness, but he simply cannot get an erection. And for me that is perfectly fine and it compensates his otherwise bad behavior.

As he's struggling to get out of the rest of his clothes, I feel a tinge of pain in my abdomen, and can't believe I might actually be getting my period.

"That's right Wells, take it all off. I'll be right back."

"You sexy little thing," his smile is picture perfect even under his heavy, sagging eyelids and bloated face.

I run-walk to the bathroom and push down my tiny black g-string and then I feel it. It *is* my period. Ugh, my day isn't going well at all. I sink down next to the sink and reach inside the cabinet and pull out a square compact like box where my diaphragm sits covered in baby powder.

Turning the water on I rinse the baby powder off, wash myself off and then sit spread eagle on top of the closed toilet lid, pushing it deep inside of me. This is a trick I learned from one of the girls when I was at the other place. And it works. The diaphragm will hold my blood and get me through the day.

To make sure he doesn't notice I spray a little perfume between my legs and then join him in the bedroom. He's managed to get naked and is sprawled out naked on the bed. His clothes are scattered like breadcrumbs across the floor.

For the next 50 minutes he entertains me with his impersonation of Elvis Presley and a story about having once gotten bottles and bottles of Chanel No. 5 for Natalie Wood to use instead of water for a luxurious sex romp in the tub. As he tells me his stories, his hand reaches for my crotch, which today I can't let him explore, so I gently push his hand away.

"Tell me what happened with the bath?" I lay my head on his shoulder, draping my leg over him, and covering his limp penis with my hand as I begin to squeeze as if it were unmolded clay.

"Well," he starts gruffly. "Thing is, when she got in, she screamed. How was I to know perfume had liquor in it? We couldn't fuck for weeks."

"Ohhh that's so funny!"

"Wasn't to her, I can tell you that," he grimaced as if remembering.

"You're still really big, Wells, bet you were huge then."

"Yeah, huge," his words are slurred closes his eyes as he thrusts his pelvis up against my hand.

He starts to moan and I join him and we're both moaning and grinding our bodies against each other.

"Fuck me Wells, fuck me."

"I'm coming, I coming!" He screams and I gently squeeze his limp penis to play along.

As I lay beside him while he regains his composure, I know he is envisioning himself coming at another time, in his previous life, because not a drop of sperm has come out of his still limp penis.

SEVEN

_____

I don't have a lot of time before the new guy Ira shows up. Normally I like changing the bed linens after every appointment. But it doesn't look like that's going to happen, and I don't feel bad about it, since Wellesley hasn't really left any trace of having been here. I straighten out the sheets, plumping up the pillows, and quietly stand in front of my closet trying to figure out what to change into.

The black dress I have on for Wellesley is pinching too much across my waist because my tummy is bloated with my soon to come period. As I scan the neatly assembled row of clothes that I keep in this apartment for work I spot dark violet strapless suede dress. I yank the expensive dress from its hanger and quickly step into it.

Scrutinizing myself in from of the full-length mirror, I decide I like the way the dress shows off my bare shoulders, and my cleavage. It's snug and cuts across my breasts sort of pushing them in and up, making them look higher and rounder and even more inviting like the women in those oversized portraits from the 18th century hanging at the Metropolitan Museum of Art.

But when I move the dress inches up my thighs because I'm bloated. I suddenly wish I had stayed home instead of coming to work today. Sighing I go back to my closet to pick out another dress and quickly take a look at the clock. It's three minutes before 1pm and I should have time to change. My hand reaches into the closet at the same time the doorbell rings.

This new guy is annoying me already. I slam the closet door shut and move on to the full-length mirror that covers the bathroom closet door. I peer closely and examine my face. The mascara looks intact. No smudges. My lipstick however needs a re-do so I quickly dab hot pink across my lips the color of a bad bridesmaid dress. I then top it off with a little gloss smack in the middle of my pouting lips.

A girl never looks tired or sad with gloss on her lips. I drop both the lipstick and gloss back into the drawer and skip-run to open the door bent at the waist fluffing out my hair, which is long past my shoulders and stops only a few inches away from the curve of my derriere. If there's anything I've learned during the time I am a call girl is how much one can do in just one or two minutes. I grab the door with one hand and push down the impossible dress which is inching up my thighs again. I inhale deeply and will myself into my sex goddess role.

The door isn't even fully open before Ira boldly pushes it away from my hand and spills into my apartment.

"Well, do come in," I say sarcastically taking a step back.

Not a good beginning for the new guy. He seems overly eager and it's off-putting.

"Good to meet you. Sorry about barging in but you never know who's behind you!" His voice is higher than it was when we spoke and he hesitates a little between his words.

"Ahhhh," he says for the first time shutting the door behind him and for a moment I think he is catching his breath. But his "ahhhs" is how he speaks and the "ahhhs" are scattered with almost every sentence until I realize he isn't aware he makes this sound when he is thinking about what to say next.

In the future when we would replay this scene in my real apartment or at a hotel anywhere in the world, he would often ask me if anyone is hiding in the closet with a camera. It always threw me off and I always thought he was weird and overly paranoid until the day arrived when I knew with certainty that people were following him and that in time I, too, would be followed.

At first blush he looks every bit the well-fed businessman in a tailor-made navy-blue pin striped suit meant to hide 30 or more extra pounds. His perfectly groomed wavy chestnut hair parted at the side is a stark contrast to his heavily hooded eyes surrounded by dark circles.

For many years into the future his first words to me will haunt me: "you never know who's behind you." Having been a trust fund kid born into the lap of luxury he was always worried about his kids being kidnapped and all sorts of strange things I only saw in mobster movies. In time I would come to know that his father Meshulam Riklis was a shady figure, who did shady things with really shady people, while amassing a fortune. He also created enemies from the underworld to the White House and sometimes it wasn't clear who was what.

Ira was familiar with all types of eavesdropping devices and different spying methods and had the habit of proudly boasting how his driver, Norman, would take a bullet for either one of his two little girls. I never knew if I was talking to one of the world's wealthiest men or to a mobster with some of the things he gabbed about. He'd gone to Wharton, the prestigious business school where his friends Michael Milken and Joe Biden had gone. So, while Ira didn't sound like a thug, he certainly thought like one.

Michael Milken

Michael Milken was indicted for the biggest Wall Street inside trading scandal in 1989. He was the head of the "junk bond" operations at Drexel Burnham Lambert. Milken learned from Meshulam Riklis complicated money transactions. In essence, the junk bond game. At Milken's sentencing the judge told him, "When a man of your power in the financial world, at the head of the most important department of one of the most important investment banking houses in this country, repeatedly conspires to violate, and violates, securities and tax laws in order to achieve more power and wealth for himself and his wealthy clients, and commits financial crimes

73

that are particularly hard to detect, a significant prison term is required."

By the time Meshulam Riklis and Michael Milken met in the 1970s he had complete control of Rapid American Corporation. It included companies like Playtex, Schenley Industries, Lerner Shops, and RKO-Stanley Warner Theatres. In 1980 Riklis took Rapid American private having worked out the details with Stanley Sporkin. Sporkin was then deputy to William "Bill" Casey as the head of the Securities and Exchange Commission (SEC). Milken's right hand man was Leon Black who went on to form the private equity firm he named Apollo. After the Jeffrey Epstein scandal of 2019 Black would become known as someone who "paid" Epstein $158 million..

Neither Black or Riklis were held responsible for their roles in the insider trading scandal that led to the bankruptcy of Drexel Burnham Lambert. It needs to be noted that it wasn't just a firm that was destroyed—the countless illegal actions irreparably damaged the financial system of the United States. Michael Milken was sentenced to 10 years in prison but served only 22 months. On October 18, 2020 then President Donald Trump pardoned Michael Milken.

Joseph Biden

Joe Biden was one of the people Ira spoke about almost more than anyone else. McCrory—a Riklis holding—had its headquarters in Philadelphia. And, so they met Biden when he was a fresh-faced aspiring politician. Joe Biden had been a Delaware Senator since he won the 1972 election. From 1987 through 1995 he served as Chairman of the Senate Judiciary Committee where he had oversight for the Department of Justice at the height of the S&L the BCCI scandals. The Bank of Credit and Commerce dubbed the Bank of Crooks and Criminals was a CIA/Mossad front.

To briefly summarize BCCI, it was founded in 1972 by Agha Hasan Abedi—a Pakistani banker. By 1991 it was defunct with 3,000 criminal customers. All of these men were involved in all manner of crimes. Gun running, narcotics, financial for nuclear weapons, money laundering—anything and everything that was illegal was done through this bank. In 1992 *Desert News* explained how this international banking criminal syndicate worked.

"There are a variety of connections between Milken, Keating, Paul and various BCCI entities that got involved in maneuvering money for the various players in the savings and loan world," [BCCI investigator Jack] Blum said. He referred to three of the largest financial scandals in the 1980s: Michael Milken and the downfall of Drexel Burnham Lambert; Charles Keating and Lincoln Savings and Loan; and Paul of CenTrust.

The book "Outlaw Bank" by Jonathan Beaty described it in the following manner.

"[A] clandestine division of the bank called the Black Network, which functions as a global intelligence operation and a mafia-like enforcement squad. The 1,500-employee Black Network has used sophisticated spy equipment and techniques, along with bribery, extortion, kidnapping and even, by some accounts, murder."

The book details some of the findings of the subsequent 1991 BCCI investigation chaired by Senator John Kerry and Senator Hank Brown. Specifically, the use of children to sexually exploit and gift to their customers.

"The protocol department [of BCCI] was also responsible for sweeping the countryside in search of another kind of prey: very young girls for the entertainment of sheikhs and Middle-Eastern businessmen.

"The wife of a Pakistani doctor was in charge of rounding up the girls and bringing them to Karachi to be outfitted in proper clothes before being presented to the princely clients. Often she would shepherd more than 50 girls at a time through a department store, shopping for jewelry and dresses. This practice was so successful—far more effective than giving away microwave ovens or toasters—that the bank would spend as much as $100,000 on such an evening's entertainment. According to the Senate testimony of Nazir Chinoy, Madam Rahim would also "interview girls, women, and take them...to Abu Dhabi for a dancing show or arrange some singing shows." Throughout the Middle East, "dancing girls" and "singing girls" are euphemisms for prostitutes."

In 1992 *The Washington Post* reported that when Senator John Kerry asked Chinoy whether 15-,-16- and 17-year-old girls were procured as prostitutes, Chinoy smiled. "Yes, sir."

Providing minor girls for BCCI's customers was the primary responsibility of the "protocol department". In

1988 they spent about $6 million employing about 450 people—among these the young girls.

Joe Biden was an influential member of the Foreign Relations Committee when it lobbied John Kerry to end the investigation into BCCI. In hindsight, when I too was a sex-slave, I wonder how many of the numerous visits the Riklis's made to Biden were connected to the BCCI affair. It should be noted that there are similarities between Michael Milken's financial crimes and those of BCCI.

~

If I had fallen into the rabbit hole when I lost my way, and ended up selling pieces of my soul by the hour, Ira's presence in my life, made me topple even deeper past any of the exit doors I might have been able to open. In decades to come, I too, would wonder who might be standing just behind me.

I double lock the front door and wrap my hand inside Ira's meaty palm leading him to the sofa where he quickly unbuttons his jacket before sitting down. I can feel his weight on my left thigh because he's sitting so close to me and I instinctively try to shuffle away, but his big clammy hand grips my thigh tight and I can't move.

His pants stretch across his wide thighs creasing the fabric and his belly pushes his crisp white shirt up and out from inside his pants where it had been neatly tucked so that he suddenly resembles an old tired man instead of the young man he is.

The routine with a new guy is vastly different than with a regular guy and I haven't had a new client in a long time, so I have to be especially careful with him. He is moving too fast and I am intent on slowing him down.

"Ira, tell me a little about yourself. What kind of business are you in?" I cross my legs and catch his eyes following the line of my leg all the way down to my black Manolo Blahnik stiletto pumps.

"I own a couple of companies that aren't exciting in the least," he gives my thigh another unwelcome squeeze.

I place my hand firmly on top of his to make sure it doesn't go any further and in the same sweet tone of voice I keep talking.

"What sort of companies?" I don't acknowledge his hand on my thigh, or the fact that my dress has betrayed me by inching up even higher so that the top of my stockings, along with the black lace of my garter belt, with my bare flesh are now visible.

"Nothing special," he's unabashedly staring at the skin between my dress and the stockings. His full lower lip dangles open. For a split second I think he is going to droll saliva all over himself.

"You are certainly the most exciting thing that's happened to me today. And maybe even for a long while," his eyes sweep up mine again and a wide grin spreads across his full face making his double chin seem even more prominent.

There is no way this guy can be a cop and so I let my guard down and intently keep my eyes locked into his now twinkling caramel colored ones punctuated by dark circles and silently give him the green light.

"I love your tie," I place my hand on it against his chest, wanting him to start feeling my touch.

"Uhmmm," he purrs. "Ahhhh…..You're lovely."

"Thank you. Come on," I stand up and make a last attempt at pushing down the hem of my dress. He presses his body close behind mine wrapping his hands around my waist so that it feels as if we are one as we walk towards the bed.

Tearing myself away from him, I recite the usual speech.

"Make yourself comfortable, and when you're ready, please leave it here." I softly tap the nightstand next to the bed. I never use the word money, not even with regulars, and especially not with a new guy. "I'll be right back."

I leave him in the room for about 4 minutes to give him time to take his clothes off and get himself ready. When I return he's completely naked and sitting comfortably on top of the cover sheet. It's hard not to notice that he's trying to suck in his rounded belly. His big legs are bent at the knee and his penis is already fully erect.

His entire demeanor tells me he has done this before. Many times. This is certainly not his first. I quickly spot his black Calvin Klein briefs and his black socks sitting neatly on top of his clothes on the chair at the foot of the bed. To me that's also another sign that he's a regular. He's someone's regular. And because he isn't a newbie, I naively believe he is going to be an easy client.

Crisp $100 bills are neatly fanned across the table and I ignore them.

His pleading eyes are glued on my body, and slowly I walk toward him. I stop a couple of inches away from his fully extended left arm with the tips of his fingers reaching out for me. Silently I undo the zipper of my dress, which thankfully is on my side, and not the back, making this little strip tease a lot easier to do.

I wiggle a little and the dress falls down to my waist. I then wiggle again, and it glides over my hips and down my legs becoming a puddle of fabric on the carpeted floor. I slowly step over it. Only black lingerie, sheer black stockings, and my black Manolo Blatnik's remain.

His eyes dart up and down all over my body, and when his eyes meet mine again, I can tell he is in the red-hot fire zone.

"Turn around let me look at you," his voice is husky with desire.

I turn around slowly stopping midpoint with my back facing him and let him take in the perfect curves of my body. My ass is perfectly round like a globe beneath my tiny waist. Standing perfectly still I turn my head sideways, narrow my Oriental-like tilted eyes, and flash him a cat-like glance.

Swirling back around, I bend down Playboy bunny style and pick up my discarded dress throwing it about carelessly about three feet away where it lands on top of his crisp white dress shirt.

Before I can even kick off my high heel shoes, I notice his plump toes are already curled and his fully erect member is visually throbbing which is in stark contrast to his perfectly still bloated body. His arms are rigid at his side and he is lying flat on his back, as if he were a soldier. Only his head is bent in my direction. His eyes are wide open and glued on me. He almost looks like he's afraid I have disappeared.

I try climbing over his big belly to get to the other side but Ira wraps his big arms around me and pulls me down tight against him. My breasts fall onto his face. His thick hands reach up and squeeze them. His mouth opens and he sucks each nipple, one at a time, for several minutes evenly. I wonder if he's trying to please himself or me as I fight to retain my balance while stuck on top of him.

To check if he is still hard, I rub my leg over his groin, and it's still fully erect. Not wanting him to climax right away I pull my leg away and try to slow him down. I push myself off him falling onto his right side and push his arm up so I can snuggle my head on his shoulder. He wraps his arm around me.

"I love the suit you were wearing," I whisper in his ear.

"Thank you, I love the dress you had on. Ahhhh…..Where did you buy it?"

"Bloomie's I think."

"Ahhh…I've always wanted to buy something off the rack. I always have to get my clothes made for me." He moans tragically.

"Why?" I free myself from his arms and prop myself up on one elbow.

"Well, because I have to lose about 20 pounds and nothing in a store ever fits me. I'm jealous that you can walk into a store and just buy something. I can't do that," he taps his protruding belly.

My eyes follow his hand, and truth be told, he could afford to lose 20 maybe even 30 or more pounds. But most men aren't in good shape. Just go to any beach and potbellied men in too-small shorts stroll by with no shame at all. A woman in the same physical condition would never go near a beach.

His full checks are flush and his eyes peer into mine. He looks tragically sad.

"You're so beautiful," he whispers caressing my face.

In response to his compliment, I run my fingers through his hair. For him it's an invitation to pull me close and kiss me on the lips. We make out as if we're on our honeymoon instead of a pay for hire hour. I pull away and straddle him.

Pushing my hair over my head and onto to his body I crawl down while my hair and skin caress him like a thousand little feathers.

He quivers under my touch.

His penis begs for my attention. I ignore it and softly lick his balls planting small kisses along his inner thighs. When I notice the drops of pre-come on his cock, I flick my tongue gently along the sides of it and within seconds he erupts onto the palm of my hand.

~

Many years from now when I stride the streets of New York as the owner of a real estate firm, when gray strands of hair find their way onto my temples, when Ira becomes independently wealthy aside from the riches bestowed upon him from him father, I will think about this day and wish I'd never given him an appointment. I would be reminded of this day whenever something bad happens to me in the future. When someone destroys my apartment or my business or my love life. I will feel overcome with a sense of both hatred and terror and I will know Ira and his goons are behind it all.

I will especially remember this when someone tries to kill me.

Many years into the future after the first attempt on my life fails, a man identifying himself as "the F.B.I." will knock on my apartment door. Although most people who visit have to buzz to gain access to the building, he doesn't. Somehow he made it through the first two doors in the lobby and is now on the other side of my door.

My nephew was with me that day and he blurted out, "Who is it?"

"F.B.I." he responded.

I never open the door. Ever. To no one since the botched attempt on my life. I tiptoe to the door and look through the peephole. He looks like he stepped out of Spy Magazine. He's tall, in his mid-30s and is wearing a trench coat. My immediate thought is that he's an actor and he's here to kill me.

"Do you have ID?" I yell through the door.

He flashes something I can't see or read and then grins like a Cheshire cat.

I feel the fear rising.

"Sorry, I received no phone call from the FBI and I don't trust you're telling me the truth. Go away or I'll call the police."

Undeterred he remains fixed outside of my apartment door and so I call the police who arrive about 12 minutes later.

I hear the elevator door open and see through the peep hole in my door the same man "FBI man" step out followed by two short police officers.

Cautiously I open the door and address the police officers.

"He showed us his I.D.," the female officer tells me.

"Ok, then please stay here while he tells me what he has to say," I respond.

"No, we have to go,"

"No, wait, please don't go," I plead and as I do I can't help but notice how amused the FBI agent is.

"Sorry, we've gotta go," they turned away and headed back into the elevator and I quickly shut the door before they disappeared inside.

"Please go away," I tell the man who isn't moving once again with the door shut closed.

"Not until I speak with you."

I run into my livingroom and find the number to the F.B.I.'s headquarters in New York City.

"Do you have an agent listed as having to speak with me?" I ask the woman who I have been transferred to.

"Give me a minute, I'll check," she says and I try to calm the beating of my heart. The thought that he is here to kill me isn't going away.

"No, we don't have anyone scheduled to speak with you."

And as a way to not sound paranoid, I add: "Thank you, I'm a woman who lives alone and I always believed your agency would have called me or sent a letter to let me know I had an appointment. I am not going to let him inside my apartment."

"Good thinking. I would advise you not to let him in either," the woman from the FBI headquarters said confirming my worst fear.

I then ignored the tall man with the trench coat on the other side of my front door and at some point he disappeared. I never again heard from anyone claiming to be from the FBI.

EIGHT

I stare myself down in the mirror, purse my lips and apply a rich, bold red lipstick. The matte red contrasts sharply with my alabaster skin. Unlike both my sisters who are sun-worshippers, I don't like sitting out in the sun letting strangers look at my body, and my skin is flawless as a result.

My older sister looks at least 50 with her fair skin lined with wrinkles. I look much younger than I am. I always have. When I was younger my wish was to look older. What was once a problem turned into an advantage. One swift dab across my lips added the mark of a woman on my seemingly young and innocent looking face. I am still nude wearing only high heeled black pumps. I always wear my high heels when making up my face because it makes me feel taller. And when I feel taller I also feel like I am more in charge. It's a small trick because if at some point I don't feel this then it's *them* who are in charge: the men. The men I hate while I tell them how perfectly wonderful they are. I brush my long thick hair that reaches just above the curve of my perfectly round ass. I know I'm pretty but that is all I know. I do not know the how's or the why's of a man's reaction to me. It has always been a mystery to me.

The hands on the clock show it's two minutes before 7am on this Tuesday morning. It's so very early. However, it is the only time Neil, one of the most powerful and expensive attorneys in New York and in Washington, D.C., can indulge his fantasies. While I hate to be call-girl ready and play the absurd games each man requires at such a ludicrous time, occasionally I indulge him. He knows he has to ask me at least six times before I agree to one 7am appointment. The fact that he always pays me three times my going rate makes it less of a struggle. Seeing him frees up my time and means I can eliminate two other appointments.

Thing is: I don't work every day. It would be impossible to do this day in and day out. I work far less days on any given month than the days I play the vixen for the men I despise.

I fasten my black seamed stockings to the satin and lace black garterbelt and then pulled on my G-string panties. This way, should things get hot, I would just push down the panties and still have the lingerie look they all like. My breasts spill over the demi cup bra exposing a glimpse of the dark area around my nipples. I grab a simple Laura Ashley dress, reminiscent of the kind of dress one wears to the country or to church on Sundays. I step into it zipping it up just as the clock hands say 7am and the doorbell rings.

Neil is small in stature but sharp of mind. He's often on TV, newspapers and magazines. He has a small mustache he must have had since his college days and it's got some grey in it. As always, he is impeccably dressed in a black suit and has an air of being a man's man. He's never one to mind words and has an unmistakable aura of power.

"Hello sweetheart," he extends his arms and takes me into his embrace, kissing me gently on my cheek. "How's my favorite girl?"

I plant a small kiss on his cheek and pull away. "I'm doing just nicely, thank you," and then I twirl around. "I bought this just for you. Do you like it?"

"I love it sugar and wait until you see what I've got." He leads the way to my bedroom and spills the contents of the paper bag onto the bed. I take a spot next to the garments and begin to lift and explore them.

"I love these!" I lie holding up two pieces, a large beige satiny bra and a pair of old-fashioned panties like the kind my mother wears.

"You don't know how excited I am about this. I went shopping for them yesterday and I could barely sleep, just thinking about this morning," As he spoke, he undressed, yanking off his suit, pulling at his perfectly made up tie with the impatience of a child, and sensing his urgency, I decide to help him. I stand inches away and unbutton the starched white shirt that is like a uniform to him. He carefully hangs up each of the garments he has removed on the expensively appointed valet I keep next to the bed.

"No use getting my suit wrinkled it might make people wonder when I get to the office later," he says this in a hurried tone like he's trying to convince himself and not me.

"Ummm, Neil," I purr, "You're going to look so sexy in these." I had him the bra and stand behind him pressing my groin against his buttocks. He moans and shivers against my touch. "Oh, you're incredible. You're so delicious!"

The game had finally begun.

"Come on, Neil, put everything on. Let's have some fun!"

One by one he took the clothes that remained on the bed and put them on. He was soon standing before me in short sleeved blouse, a short A-lined skirt and a pair of sheer stockings he attached to what looked like an oversized garterbelt.

"How do I look?" he asked like a little girl standing next to the bed in his stockinged feet.

"You look great. Now put the shoes on," I urge daintily.

The gracefulness of the man disappeared as he held on to my shoulder and stumbled into the pair of black low-rise heels that normally women who have never been married wear. His eyes met mine for approval and his eyebrows arched higher.

"Yes, they're wonderful." It was time to get this done so he could leave. "We girls, you know," I pause so I can say it again. "We girls have to stick together." I gently push him down onto the bed and leave my hand on his knee.

His voice had become lighter, softer, as he murmured in agreement.

"Ohhh, what are you doing?" He asked in a bashful tone as I slid my hand up his thigh lightly touching the satiny panties.

"Tell me the color of your panties," I state sternly as if I hadn't watched him dress. "What color are they, tell me." I could feel his body quiver with anticipation.

"An off white, I think," he says meekly.

"Ummmm, I like that. Let me feel them." It's not really a question but a comment because I begin to grope him and cup his balls into the palm of my hand. My fingers begin to trail along the elastic of his oversized panties and then rest my palm again this time on the hardness of his cock.

"Ohhhh, are you touching my pussy? Are you touching my pussy?" He repeats, his voice is high and barely recognizable as the man he is. He has completely disappeared into his fantasy world and he's lost to the ecstasy.

He begins to touch me as I am touching him, and we're soon locked into a tangle of arms and legs, while we're still fully dressed.

"You're so beautiful,' I say to him echoing what so many have whispered to me while I unbutton his blouse and push up his bra exposing his nipples. I lick and take them into my mouth and they become erect, engorged with blood. He grabs my breasts and pulls me up hiding his face between them. The Laura Ashley dress opens up seamlessly for his to suckle on my breasts now fully exposed. He slurps like he is a hungry child suckling milk.

I push him off and let the dress fall off me and onto the floor and then I straddle him gyrating on his hardness through our panties. He is rock hard and I know he is ready.

"Let's rub our breasts together," he begs and we do. He's pushed the old-fashioned bra way up where it sits below his velvety smooth chin. His hairy chest looks weirdly out of place under the layers of women's clothes. Like a zebra in a room full of horses. I glance at the clock and push down my panties so he could at least feel me without going inside and I push down his panties so I could straddle his dick against the lips of my pussy. Almost immediately he explodes.

"I'm coming! I'm coming!" he yells as his body convulses.

Before the hour Neil was gone and I needed to have a second cup of coffee. This last encounter while not entire crazy was really too much play acting for me. His lesbian fantasy required a lot of work. It is time to blacklist him.

NINE

"It's me," Ira's shrill voice slices into the small apartment from the answering machine on what I'd hoped would be a calm start to the week. "I'd like to see you again. Monday 11:00 o'clock." It isn't a question, but rather a statement. His voice and arrogance irritate me. My finger quickly jabs at the machine and turns it off. Ira's desired time slot is taken and he hasn't left a number where he can be reached. A flash of anger along with a new level of vulnerability invades my body.

Breathe in, exhale. Breathe in, exhale. Breathe in, exhale. I have to remain composed to make it through my day.

One day in the near future Ira will confess that during that first weekend after we met, he dialed my number with fiendish frenzy over 100 times. And, that he'd snuck off to fantasize about me, after having lunch with his wife and children at Rumplemeyer's, under the pretense that he had work to do.

Like a hormone crazed teenage boy, he holes himself up in his lavishly appointed private office on the 18th floor at the glitzy Trump Tower, where the family-run Rapid American billion-dollar conglomerate occupies both the 18th and 25th floors and jerks off while thinking about me.

All around the city, women my age are embarking on their professional careers or beginning their young married lives. Their world is mixture of work, boyfriends, weddings, babies, social outings with friends, newfound loves; along with the excited anticipation of everything new that lays before them. Life for them is predictable and normal.

For me, nothing is normal, and with Ira, I will enter into a parallel universe, freakier even than the one I have fallen into. For decades to come my life will be a series of one unpredictable event after another. What I do not know is that Riklis has already become the conductor of my life. For decades he will pull off elaborate behind the scenes machinations that will toss me about as if I were the shrunken Alice in the children's fantasy book.

There is an unwritten code for call girls in New York City about canceling appointment: it is not done. It's okay to rush a guy while he's with you and have him to leave earlier than he might otherwise want to, but to altogether cancel a highly anticipated appointment places a girl at risk of losing a trusted client.

Willing myself into character I pick up the phone. "I am sick," I lie sweetly. "I'll make it up to you," I promise as his disappointed voice fades away.

Something has gone horribly and irrevocably wrong with my life. It bears no resemblance at all to 'my life' anymore. I have stopped being an aspiring designer and have become instead a call girl. Random series of events have altered my life in a way that makes absolutely no sense to me. I am at the core of my being a good girl. I don't sleep around when I am not in this make-believe apartment. Before being thrust into this world, I had a steady boyfriend, was a good student, had real aspirations, didn't wear anything overly revealing, and was frankly, rather shy.

I give myself the once over in the mirror just before opening the door and the reflection of a well put together woman in a white Thierry Mugler suit looks back at me. The image bears little resemblance to who I remember I was.

The snug jacket with rhinestone buttons flares out dramatically accentuating my narrow waist. The skirt fits snuggly around my hips and it stops three inches above my knees. My legs are covered in white fishnet stockings and I am 4 inches taller than I normally am in white patent leather t-strap stilettos. My hair is teased giving it just the right amount of tousled sexy. On the bathroom sink sinks a large red can of Aqua Net hairspray. I hold the can firm in one hand and spritz it all over my hair while squeezing my eyes shut. Spray, spray, spray – the smell of hairspray permeates the tiny apartment freezing my hair firmly in place.

In the future while sitting next to Ira in the back of a black limousine on our way to Philadelphia we will make a pit stop at a convenience store because I have forgotten to pack my hairspray. Rushing back into the car with a small can of Aqua Net, he will say to me, "we make twenty-five cents on each one of these."

～

In the book *The Go-Go Years: The Drama and Crashing Finale of Wall Street's Bullish 60s* written by John Brooks, he writes of Rapid American's creator:

"Meshulam Riklis, born in Odessa grew up in pre-Israel Tel Aviv in comfortable circumstances, making

such frequent and intricate deals with his playmates that they took to calling him derisively the Minister of Finance. He was no ordinary Jewish boy, but it was sometimes maintained, an eighth-generation descendant of Baal-Shem-Tov, founder in eighteenth-century Poland of the celebrated ultra-orthodox Jewish sect called Hasidism. Nonreligious like his father—a Palestine businessman who had once been an officer in the Turkish army—Meshulam Riklis showed an early bent toward scholarship, leading his mother to hope fervently that he would get a Ph.D. and become a teacher. He did, for a time, become a teacher. Having served in the British army in wartime and later having lived for a while with his bride in a kibbutz, he came to the United States in 1947, graduated from Ohio State University in 1950, and then moved to Minneapolis, where he taught Hebrew at night and spent his days as a novice stock salesman for a local brokerage firm.

At the daytime occupation he made a quick success. Soon the rich Zionists of Minneapolis were willing to finance him in independent ventures, and he began buying and combining small companies on a shoestring. He would line up backers to help him get control of Company A; then he would use the assets of Company A to take over Company B; and so on. In 1955 he took over a firm called American Colortype; and the combination, which was to be Riklis' key corporate vehicle thereafter, he named Rapid-American Corporation—a name so inspiring, so beautifully characteristic of the air of guileless enthusiasm seasoned with amiable larceny of the conglomerate era, that it must endear him to any student of corporate nomenclature.

Naturalized in 1955 and a millionaire before the end of that decade, Riklis was Rapid-American in the flesh. In 1970 he told a reporter, "I am a conglomerate. Me personally." By 1962 his Rapid-American controlled McCrory Corporation, a combine of retail stores, and Glen Alden, a consumer-products company.

Eventually Riklis came to control a complex with sales of $1.7 billion, including such well-known companies as International Playtex, B.V.D., Schenley Industries, Lerner Shops, and RKO-Stanley Warner Theatres."

When I researched Ira's father a bit more I discovered that he had been regarded as a math wizard. In an interview he gave to the *LA Times* in 1986 he said he worked for the brokerage firm Piper, Jaffray & Hopwood in Minneapolis. That it was at this firm, where he was "the only Jew" where he raised from his brokerage clients $750,000 in 1954 for his first deal. He used that money to acquire Gruen Watch of Cincinnati and called it a "sleeping beauty" because its stock was selling for less than the cash in its till.

~

I don't know who Ira is at this point in time, and even if I had known, it would have made no difference. To me he is a wicked quick fly in need of a good swift swat.

His bulky frame marches in confidently.

"You're not an easy girl to forget," he chirps his twinkling brown eyes roaming the length of me before he opens his arms for a hug. A small blue Tiffany bag dangles from one of his plump hands.

"That's not a good excuse, it's a nice compliment, but not a good excuse. You have to make an appointment. You really cannot just show up here whenever you want." My face doesn't betray how peeved I really feel as I shut the door and bury my check into his shoulder surrendering to his embrace.

I pull away and he drops a kiss on my lips in a perfunctory way as if he were my lover.

"I've been calling you all weekend, where have you *been*?" He emphasizes the word 'been' in the same manner a child whines when he can't have another cookie.

"I've been busy."

"By the way this is for you," he hands me the bag, a wide grin distorts his full face, as he looks at me with boyish anticipation.

"Thank you. You really don't have to buy me anything," I peek inside expecting to see a small blue box tied with Tiffany's signature white ribbon but find instead a stack of $100 bills.

"What is this?" We're glued by the front door in my work apartment. It faces the front and it's noisy. Jarring sirens, honking horns and bracing brakes compete for attention alongside Miles Davis' Sketches of Spain, which I have put into the cassette player for his appointment. It's a bedlam of noise most New Yorkers become oblivious to.

"Ahhhh," he tilts his head back and stares up at the ceiling. I notice short stubbles of beard alongside his neck and face under red patches of skin indicating he shaved this morning.

"Well…I would have preferred to buy you a piece of jewelry from Harry Winston but I didn't see you wear any jewelry last time. I wasn't sure what your style might be so I thought you could go out and get yourself something you liked." He says the name Harry Winston as if it were four words: HA-rry Win-Ston.

"Thank you, really, you didn't have to get me anything," my anger disappears as I ponder the idea of not working for a week or two depending on how much is in the bag. I only work when I have to pay bills. Depending on how much money is in the bag, I may not have to work for a little while.

"Consider it my gift to you," he responds magnanimously.

Before I can respond, he scoops me up in his arms, kisses me passionately muttering how much he's missed me, and carries me off into the bedroom. Lowering me gently on the bed he kneels down on the floor beside me.

I start unbuttoning my jacket, but he quickly grabs my hands.

"No, I'm going to take your clothes off," he instructs feverishly, his face getting puffy with desire.

Slowly he removes every stitch of clothing carefully placing each item on the chair at the foot of the bed. And in less than two minutes, gone too, are the stockings, garter-belt and matching g-string, which I'd planned on wearing throughout his appointment.

His eyes narrow like slits and he stars hard at me from a sunken pool of darkness. The dark circles under his eyes look even more pronounced and I wonder if he's gotten any sleep.

"It's your turn," I am as naked as Edouard Manet's *'Olympia'* and fluff up the pillows before reclining on them. This has become quite the upside-down appointment and I just want it to be over. He's the one that is supposed to be fully naked by now, not me.

With several loud guttural heaves, he gets up off his knees and stands. Impatiently he discards his impeccably tailored suit and tosses all his clothes on a heap onto the chair.

I feel the bed dip next to me as he climbs in. His cold feet brush against mine as he straddles me. The bed creaks ominously as he grabs both my hands into his large sweaty palms and pins my arms back over my head.

His face hovers over me. It's slack and damp with sweat, Awkwardly, he presses his half open mouth hard against my lips. I shut my eyes and let his tongue slip into mine.

I can't breathe. I am being smothered alive. Jerking my head to the right I free myself from his death kiss.

"No, don't do that," he instructs hoarsely. We're in battle.

He repositions himself alongside of my legs, his eyes droopy with desire, and pushes my legs apart. Bouncing heavily across the mattress he sits between my legs and stares at my vagina as if he's never seen one before. His thick fingers jab at my clitoris. Mistaking my cries for pleasure he rubs me faster and faster, harder and harder, back and forth.

I am writhing in pain, but he's glowing with self-satisfaction and is oblivious to the excruciating pain he has inflicted upon me. Does he really think I am having an orgasm?

The 1980s gave birth to the word G-spot and for years to come Ira will remain obsessed with finding mine. "No, no, stop, stop!" I shriek swatting away at his hands.

Whatever I do, I can't tell him he's not pleasing me. Some clients feel it's their manly duty to make you happy in bed. And I can't tell if that's what he's trying to do or whether he gets off on hurting me.

Like a dagger his middle finger plunges deep into me. Deeper and deeper he tries to push. Pulling away from his assault I find myself sitting against the headboard.

His face is euphoric as he looks at me triumphantly.

I push him off me and he lands against the oversized pillows.

Just as I am about to get him off, so he can leave, he starts talking.

"Ahhh," he stammers. "I've never gone all the way with anyone but my wife."

'No kidding' I think sarcastically after the catastrophic sex. I'm sore and all I want is for him to leave.

Instead I snuggle onto his chest since I know he's going to need a few minutes before he can get it up again and he wraps his arms around me.

"What do you mean?" I tilt my head up to his and he begins rattling off the most intimate details of his sex life.

"Well, ahhhh…I've seen ladies, of course, but I've never made love to any of them. Never wanted to. But lately, all I can think of is how much I want to make love to you. To hold you in my arms and never let go."

"You've been thinking about me?" I ask playfully placing my bare leg across his in an attempt to tease an erection out of him.

"Yes, a lot. There's something about you….ahhhh…..that's quite special. I've never seen it before. It reminds me of the first time I met my wife. It scares me and you are exactly what my wife, is terrified of.

"What do you mean?"

"When we go to Europe, she seems to know I'm going to do something and it's okay there. But not here. She would be very scared of you and of how I am feeling for you."

Not wanting to hear him talk about his wife fearing it would interfere with him having an erection that would enable me to get him to leave I change the subject.

"Hey, let's not go down that road."

Men are undeniably different than women. In their minds if they pay for sex, they don't think they're really cheating. And, apparently, in Ira's mind the fact that his penis has never penetrated another woman makes him feel as if he's been a faithful husband.

In the midst of what is only a performance Ira then shifts from talking about his wife and begins ranting about his troubles with his father. A torrential downpour of hurt feelings mixed with self-doubt stream out of him.

"My father isn't too pleased....He wants absolute control over me....He sees me as a something that belongs to him....Like one of his companies....Didn't want me to get married....Now they're the best of friends....I think he's calling the house to speak with me, but it's her he wants to talk to....He spoils the children....We have a power struggle....He never hugs me....I thought I was gay..." his words tumble out of him interspersed with his "Ahhhhhs."

I wait until he calms down and then move up close to his ear taking his earlobe into my mouth and bite it softly.

He moans and as he does his penis gets hard again.

I straddle him with his manhood flat under my sore vagina so that he doesn't slip in. Slowly I begin to gyrate. I can feel him pulsate beneath me. Within seconds his body stiffens and his arms flail by his side. I jump off as he grabs himself ejaculating all over his bloated belly.

TEN

During our third and final time in our roles as 'The Call Girl and The Billionaire,' Ira takes the time and effort to book a real appointment. I'd been set on never seeing him again and was ready to blacklist him if he hadn't shown me the slight courtesy of following my rules.

His serious brown eyes stare deep into my own and happy to be near me his face is bright and beaming as spreads out across my bed. His left arm dangles off the side of the bed and he holds me snug against his shoulder with his right. Too tightly, too close for my comfort, but I focus on the fact that he will be gone shortly and so I ignore the momentary annoyance and discomfort.

"Do you know why I don't wear my watch on my right wrist?" he asks and I know he just wants to make conversation.

"No, why?" I didn't really care and hadn't really noticed that he wore his watch on the left wrist. He always took his watch off before climbing into bed anyway. I insisted on day one so that it wouldn't snag into my hair which I preferred wearing around my shoulders and down my back.

"Because I had a skiing accident," he began and while I wasn't really intensely listening I looked up at him to make it look like I was really interested. That is after all why any of these men come to girls like me. One hundred percent attention. They don't get this at home or with any normal woman.

A smile spreads across his cherub checks making an adult case of mild acne even more noticeable. With a soft moan he pulls me even closer to him, and pushes a long strand of hair away from my face. "You need a vacation. Why don't you accept a gift from me and go on a cruise?"

I cannot believe this man who appears to be somewhat intelligence, being so wealthy and all believes he is here with me because I want him here. I really should not let him linger holding me the way he does. But I decide to go with flow since he's a one-time Charlie meaning he is a one-climax-per-visit-man. Some of these otherwise well-mannered men will try to squeeze in a second go, but he hadn't, and so I let him blather away.

"No thanks, I'd be bored being on a ship with the same people day after day." What I really meant was that I wasn't going to be taking a gift from him or any other of my clients. I didn't want to feel indebted to anyone. I saw who I wanted to see and when they became too difficult, I'd stop seeing them altogether. Taking gifts makes a girl sloppy and closes off her options.

Plus, I was already getting really tired of this life. Whether it was burn out or the deep desire I had to live like normal people, I knew I couldn't pull this act off for much longer. It took all my time and all my energy to turn into everyone's fantasy woman. Like *'The Stepford Wives'* film with all the women looking perfect and fulfilling every desire of their husbands. In the movie the men have really disposed of their wives and have replaced them with robots. I was still a real woman with real feelings that I suppressed for every one of these men.

"I insist. Really, it'll do you, ahhh, good. Carnival Cruise Lines is part of my family business, so I'll be giving you something while keeping it all in the family at the, ahhh, same time."

Even in the mid-1980s Carnival wasn't high on anyone's list and I was somewhat put off. Frankly I would have said no to a cruise on the Queen Mary, but Carnival definitely had an ick factor.

"No thanks. So where are you off to now?" Which was my way of saying "time's up".

While he's getting dressed, he stops, gives me a deep look, forgets about buttoning up his crisp white shirt and pulls me close to him. Hoarsely, he whispers into my ear: "I love you. I never thought I'd feel this way about another woman but I do. I love you."

He looks incredibly sincere and I've been in this situation before. There are men who don't see the invisible line that separates them from the illusion I've created. The person they see does not exist—she's merely my job. While I don't doubt his sincerity I also don't want to lead him on. Breaking the silent code of never discussing their wives, I bring her up instantly as a way of letting him know to 'STOP!"

"You're married," I snap pushing him away while reminding him of the obvious.

"Yes, and I've known her since I was fourteen. I never thought I would meet someone I'd leave her for. You know," he begins earnestly, "when my father left my mother and married Pia Zadora, I was so angry with him. It was more than the divorce. It was marrying outside the Jewish religion. But I can see why he did it now. I understand it because of you. I'd leave her for you, if you'd have me."

My head felt like it was in a vice. I listened until he ran out of things to say and then showed him to the door, dutifully kissed him goodbye and wished him a nice day.

In the short period of time I'd known Ira, all he did when he spoke about the women in his life was to demolish them. He was either complaining about his wife's nagging, to putting down her friends for being skeletal thin, or saying malicious things about his father's wife, Pia Zadora, for being what he termed a gold-digger. At each point, I would try to point out that so and so wasn't this or that. In Pia's case, I told him that she'd helped his father get back on top. His response was, "That's because top for her was bottom for my him. It's all in what you have when you enter the game."

~

I'd had the phones turned off while he was in the apartment and decided to leave them that way. I hadn't put Ira into my black book. And now that he'd been so persistent and I'd seen him three times I figured he was already a regular. I fished for my book in the kitchen cupboard behind the assorted cans of coffee. I was so paranoid about anyone finding out what I did that I cleaned the apartment myself. I longed to hire a cleaning woman but I did not want anyone to notice what I was doing; and for sure, anyone cleaning up my apartment would notice a lot of things were off.

My life was riddled with secrets. I lay the book onto the counter and thumbed through to the letter "I". I then scribbled "Ira Riklis, late 20s or 30s, married, two children, both girls, lost their third child before birth, no fucking, one-time climax," and then added 9/11 as the first time we'd met. I made some additional notations with the clothes I'd worn so that I wouldn't wear the same outfit twice. I was very meticulous about what I wore for each client. I then flipped the pages to "N" and found Neal's name. I wrote a giant 'X' so that I'd remember I blacklisted him.

ELEVEN

Over twenty years later I'd write about Carnival Cruise, LLC and my recollection of that day when the Costa Concordia sank on January 13, 2012. My article appeared in a couple of newspapers and I believe is still on a cruise line website. I include it here with my memoir because connecting the dots is always a good thing when remembering the past. Especially when one is writing about well-known people and events that changed the course of history.

In my experience, the clues to a man are sometimes right out in the open in the ways they run their companies. In the way their close friends run their companies. In the way they have complete disregard for the lives of ordinary people. People like myself and like you.

In response to the largest passenger ship disaster since the sinking of the Titanic 100 years ago, Carnival Corp (CCL), has placed the blame entirely on Capt. Francesco Schettino. A spokesperson for the company stated that Schettino made an "unapproved, unauthorized" deviation in the course of the Costa Concordia whose hull was torn open on Friday 13th when the ship struck rocks off the island of Giglio, Italy.

As survivors speak angrily about their horrifying ordeal, images eerily similar to those seen in the movie Titanic have emerged. Sandra Rogers a 62-year-old grandmother from Minorca told a reporter from the Daily Mail: "There was no women and children first policy. There were big men, crew members, pushing their way past us to get into the lifeboats."

Carnival Corp (CCL) claims the partial sinking of the Concordia will cost them approximately $85 million to $95 million in lost earnings for the year. When compared to the $6.5 million dollars Carnival paid for their first ship in 1972 one can safely conclude the company which now owns over 100 passenger ships has deep enough pockets and insurance to absorb this loss.

The origin and rise of the largest cruise company in the world is rooted in what some might call murky waters.

Meshulam Riklis and Ted Arison (born Theodore Arisohn) founded Carnival Cruise Lines. The pair became friends in Tel Aviv (the then British Mandate of Palestine) while attending school during the early 1940s. In 1971 Arison approached Riklis who owned, among other businesses, American International Travel Services (AITS) of Boston, to help him get back into the cruise business.

Two previous ventures had soured for Arison. In 1968 the Israeli government impounded his small cruise ship for unpaid fines. Instead of paying the money to retrieve his ship, and because he may not have had the money, he abandoned it. Just as quickly, however, Arison transferred all the passengers onto another ship. The second mishap happened in 1971 after when he had a nasty falling out with his Norwegian Caribbean Cruise Line (NCL) partner Knut Kloster. Kloster canceled his contract with Arison, who had promised profits of at least $1.5 million dollars. When Kloster's share during the second year of their partnership failed to reach that number, he severed his ties with Arison. He immediately

117

seized the advance money from all the NCL offices across the country and then filed a lawsuit against Klostner. During the time of the lawsuit, Arison used one million of the "seized" funds and began a new cruise line.

Riklis and Arison had more than just a school in Israel in common. They both earned well deserved reputations of being ruthless barracudas in their primal pursuit of financial gain.

The enterprising Riklis-Arison duo purchased *Empress of Canada* from Canadian Pacific for $6.5 million—using Riklis's money—and renamed the ship *Mardi Gras*. On its maiden voyage it ran aground with approximately 500 people on board before it ever left Miami.

CARNIVAL CRUISE'S MAIDEN VOYAGE IN 1972 TURNS BOTCHED CRUISE INTO A PUBLICITY STUNT

In February of 1973 Riklis used AITS to purchase the Riviera Hotel in Las Vegas for $56 million. The hotel had ties to infamous mobster Meyer Lansky. The Nevada Gaming Commission had Riklis dispose of its interests in Carnival or lose the hotel's gaming license. Riklis and Arison exchanged a document whereby Riklis sold his 50% share in Carnival for $1. People familiar with the transaction believe the Riklis family still own a portion of Carnival. But nothing really changed. Ira told me the mobsters were their partners in Las Vegas and that his family still owned Carnival.

Carnival Corp. (as it is known today) became the mega giant it is by registering their ships in foreign countries in order to avoid paying U.S. taxes. The company is also notoriously known to exploit Third World laborers who work on their ships for slave wages. A recent lawsuit by a former employee shows the company paid him a paltry $1.70 per hour. Their lobbyists, on the other hand, receive a small fortune to ensure tax laws don't change in Congress.

On October 8, 1999, almost 10 years after Arison denounced his U.S. citizenship and returned to Israel in an effort to avoid paying estate and inheritance taxes, he passed away of a heart attack at the age of 75.

Arison's son Micky (owner of Miami Heat) became Carnival's CEO. In 2012 Micky's net worth was estimated at $4.5 billion (after dropping $1.3 billion) according to Forbes Magazine.

His daughter Shari Arison inherited one-third of his wealth making her the richest woman in Israel. Among her holdings $3.7 billion from Carnival Corp., $698 million from Bank Hapoalim, $90 million from Housing & Construction holdings, plus a $500 million endowment from the Ted Arison Foundation.

In 2002 Forbes Magazine reported that Meshulam Riklis left his business creditors holding the bag for approximately $4 billion. The companies included the Riviera, McCrory Corp., McCrory Parent Corp., E-II Holdings and Dylex.

In 2010, a then 86-year-old Meshulam Riklis married 51-year-old Tali Sinai. When asked exactly how much he was worth by a reporter, the billionaire replied: "What difference does it make? I can only wear one pair of shoes at a time." He didn't, of course, mean that: money is all that mattered to him.

His son, Ira Riklis, told this writer on numerous occasions that his father worked hard on staying off the Forbes 400.

And confirming speculation that the Riklis family were still co-owners of Carnival Corp, in the mid-1980s Ira Riklis offered me a free vacation on Carnival telling me at the time "you need a vacation and, after all, it's a family business. And, you gotta keep it in the family".

To purchase the mob-entrenched Riviera in 1973 Riklis used $56 million from the Nevada Employees Retirement System—since he did not believe in using his own cash.

The Riviera was one of Las Vegas's premier destination spots with members of the Rat Pack, Frank Sinatra, Dean Martin and Sammy Davis Jr., all headlining. Behind the scenes it was home to the Chicago mobsters.

The Chicago crime family is part of the larger Italian-American Mafia. It's leader was Al Capone. They rose to power in the 1920 distributing illegal alcohol during prohibition. Capone got his start as a hitman.

Tony Accardo, known as "Joe Batters" was the boss during the time Riklis started his operation Las Vegas operation. He got his nickname from Capone who having watched him use a baseball bat to murder three mobsters was quoted as saying, "Boy, this kid's a real Joe Batters." Accardo was heard boasting on federal wiretaps that he participated in the infamous 1929 St. Valentine's Massacre with Capone.

The Riviera opened their doors in 1955 at a time when all five organized crime families had sunken their teeth and their claws into the casinos a decade earlier. Gambling profits were skimmed and sent back to their bosses with even more skimming before it reached its final destination. There was illegal betting, drug running, prostitution, murders and everything in between.

Three of the most famous movies used The Riviera – the original 1960 *Ocean's 11* featuring Rat Pack members Peter Lawford, Frank Sinatra, Dean Martin, Sammy Davis Jr., and Joey Bishop; the 1971 James Bond film *Diamonds are Forever*, and the 1995 movie based on real life mobsters Frank Rosenthal and Anthony Spilotro in *Casino* with Robert De Niro, Sharon Stone, Joe Pesci, Don Rickles, Kevin Pollak and James Woods.

The Riviera had so many mob killings it was believed by the hotel workers to have been haunted. They claimed to have heard voices in the stairwells and felt the presence of ghosts while they were cleaning the top-floor suites.

During my time with Ira Riklis he told me that his father, Meshulam Riklis, and the mob had a partnership at the Riviera in Las Vegas. This partnership did nothing to deter the Riklis's from being involved in the lives of the politicians. Or from being invited to White House functions. Or from having one of their companies, Playtex, selected to make the spacesuits worn by Neil Armstrong and Buzz Aldrin in the historic 1969 Apollo 11 mission. It always seemed odd to me that Playtex known for their cheap bras was trusted with the task of making the gear that made it possible for the astronauts to go to the moon. NASA describes them as a "unique blend of technology and tailoring".

Twelve

Rapid-American Corporation, the conglomerate created by Meshulam Riklis, and the vehicle which made him and his family multi-billionaires, filed for bankruptcy on March 2013. The company cited an increase in the number of Mesothelioma, asbestos, and wrongful death claims filed against it, as well as an increase in the dollar amount to settle the claims, according to court documents.

What most shareholders, and even people close to the Riklis family didn't know was that Rapid-American

Corporation also owned Philip Carey Manufacturing Corp. Philip Carey produced insulation materials for boilers, pipes and other industrial equipment. They obtained the asbestos they needed to make their products from the Quebec Asbestos Mining Company. It wasn't until the 1970s that scientists declared it a toxic material unsafe for human contact.

Rapid-American Corporation was first sued for asbestos related injuries in 1974. Riklis then employed a tactic he and his family have used many times using one corporate entity to hide another corporate entity – bottom line to hide the real owners from any legal liability.

Celotex Corporation, owned by Rapid-American (although Jim Walker's name also appears as the owner of the company – which is exactly what has kept the Riklis family in the background of the ever growing personal injury lawsuits across the country) – became the only entity to handle lawsuits filed against the Philip Carey Corporation.

MESHULAM RIKLIS QUOTE AS TOLD TO BUSINESS WEEK IN 1974

"If you are a Rockefeller or a hotel owner, you build an empire based on the company's worth," he told Business Week in 1974 when the magazine asked about his mounting debt. "If you are Meshulam Riklis, you build an empire using every possible trick."

The Celotex ploy worked indemnifying Rapid-American during the mid-1980s to late 1990. During this period Celotex fought savagely against all lawsuits to the point of counter-suing claimants. When it could not make some lawsuits disappear the company then offered very small settlements. In 1990 Riklis sought protection by filing bankruptcy for Celotex at which time a trust fund was established; however, lawsuits now fell onto Rapid-American directly.

As a side note: In 2003 the Celotex Asbestos Settlement Trust paid New York City for property damages of schools and buildings based on over 400 claims. The trustees attempted to deny payments, but were ordered by the court to make payments in excess of $40 million.

The history of Rapid-American Corp began in 1955 when Riklis took control of a company called Rapid Electrotype. In 1957 he then merged this with another company he took control over named American Colortype. From these two office equipment companies, he created the corporate vehicle Rapid-American, a name that was sufficiently ambiguous to serve whatever purpose Riklis might have in mind.

And for 56 years, it was.

Rapid-American would add many companies to its holdings such as International Playtex, Schenley Industries, Lerner Shops, RKO-Stanley Warner Theatres, McCrory's, Leeds Travelware, Gruen Watch Company, Elizabeth Arden, Aunt Nellie's Farm Kitchen's Bargain Time, Beatrice Foods, Faberge Cosmetics, J.J. Newberry stores, Lawry's Meat Specialties, Martha White Foods, Odd Lot Trading, Samsonite, The Riviera, Carnival Cruise, Canadian retailer Dylex, and Glen Alden which was the holding company for Philip Carey and the other asbestos related companies like Celotex.

In formal terms, Riklis was Rapid's largest shareholder--but not its only one. There were thousands of investors who had bought its stock on the open market. Nevertheless, he was often charged with running the company virtually as a private preserve, mixing his personal investments with Rapid business as if it were all one and all his.

In 1978, the mixing of Riklis and Rapid affairs had become so thorough that the SEC hauled him in for lengthy testimony about his financial condition, which Riklis delivered as if from the bottom of a very, very deep financial hole. He owed $60 million, personally, because of his private investments. The SEC sued him for a series of transactions in which he sold off parts of Rapid to pay down its debt, then took personal loans from the buyers to help pay down his own debt. Riklis agreed to an injunction forcing him to separate Rapid's affairs from his multitudinous private deals. From this point on he nursed a sour view of the typical stockholder as being some five-share owner who bought into the Riklis vision, only to start grousing and second-guessing. Three years later, he rid himself of these shareholders by taking Rapid private.

By 2001 Forbes would write of Riklis: "The Beverly Hills financier made and lost fortunes using leveraged buyouts that left bondholders with little…There's frequently a bankruptcy along the way." Bottom line he fleeced the companies dry.

Riklis is also credited with being one of the corporate raiders who, during the 1980s, was among men who walked away with an estimated $2.1 billion earmarked for workers' retirement accounts; and this is just what has been publicly stated. The book *Betrayal of the American Dream* by Donald Barlett and James Steele, is a must read to see how American workers who have toiled for a lifetime are left with nothing as crooks like Meshulam Riklis continue to live lavishly. It is the story of how the American middle class has been methodically impoverished and thwarted from achieving the American dream in favor of a new ruling class: the elite.

PROLOGUE

The Betrayal of the American Dream is the story of how a small number of people in power have deliberately put in place policies that have enriched themselves while cutting the ground out from underneath America's greatest asset—its middle class.

Their actions, going back more than three decades, have relegated untold numbers of American men and women to the economic scrap heap—to lives of reduced earnings, chronic job insecurity, and a retirement with fewer and fewer benefits. Millions have lost their jobs. Others have lost their homes. Nearly all face an uncertain future. Astonishingly, this has been carried out in what is considered the world's greatest democracy, where the will of the people is supposed to prevail. It no longer does. America is now ruled by the few—the wealthy and the powerful who have become this country's ruling class.

This book tells how this has happened, who engineered the policies that are crippling the middle class, what the consequences will be if we fail to reverse course, and what must be done to restore the promise of the American dream.

The biggest winners under the bill weren't working Americans, however, but money men. Congress wrote the law so broadly that it allowed corporate raiders to dip into pension funds and remove cash set aside for workers' retirement. During the 1980s, that's exactly what a cast of corporate raiders, speculators, Wall Street buyout firms, and company executives did with a vengeance, walking away with an estimated $21 billion earmarked for workers' retirement pay. The raiders insisted that they took only excess assets that weren't needed.

Among the pension buccaneers: Meshulam Riklis, the onetime partner of Carnival Cruise founder Ted Arison. A takeover artist, Riklis skimmed millions from several companies, including the McCrory Corporation, the former retail fixture of Middle America that is now gone; and the late Victor Posner, the Miami Beach corporate raider who siphoned millions of dollars from more than half a dozen different companies, including Fischbach Corporation, a New York electrical contractor that he drove to the edge of extinction. Those two raiders alone raked off about $100 million in workers' retirement dollars—all perfectly legal, courtesy of Congress. By the time billions of dollars were gone and the public outcry so loud that even Congress could not ignore it, lawmakers in 1990 rewrote the rules and imposed an excise tax on money

129

The Riklis's sumptuous lifestyles consists of full-time chauffeurs, full time nannies, private planes (Meshulam Riklis had a fleet of seven; while his son Ira Riklis recently purchased two – a Flexjet and a Learjet); art collections that would make most museums blush, along with personal homes whose cumulative price tags could run entire countries.

For example, in 1988 Riklis, then married to Pia Zadora, purchased the Pickfair mansion which they completely demolished and rebuilt. The estate is on the market today for $60 million. His New York City digs, a five-story 1880s townhouse at 17 East 75th Street, cost Riklis $4.55 million. It is listed under 'Zadora Enterprises' with an address at 725 Fifth Avenue which is Trump Tower. Another $13 million was spent on renovating the home with elaborate gold-and-marble bathrooms, a greenhouse, a $1 million black marble central staircase, all new plumbing and wiring along with a new 10 by 15-foot skylight. Riklis purchased the private home from Phyllis McGuire - one of the McGuire Sisters and Sam Giancana's ex-girlfriend. An interesting backstory on the house can be found in Dominique Dunne's "The Mansions of Limbo" where he wrote:

"...not mentioning Sam Giancana when writing about Phyllis McGuire would be like not mentioned Richard Burton when writing about Elizabeth Taylor."

In their famous showplace, America's ex-sweetheart and America's ex-boyfriend reign over Hollywood

In 1947 Pickfair was dubbed by *Life Magazine* as "a gathering place only slightly less important than the White House...and much more fun." Even members of the Royal family such as Lord and Lady Mountbatten were frequent guests. Douglas Fairbanks and Mary Pickford purchased the property in 1918.

Ira Riklis, his son, owns several homes, one of them on Park Avenue, which is valued at more than $20 million (for just the one apartment), with second homes on Long Island and in New Jersey.

Meshulam Riklis's deceased daughter, Mona Riklis Ackerman, owned a Fifth Avenue apartment once owned by Barbara Hutton. New York's social diary would say of Mona's December 19, 2006 holiday party:

131

"Mona's was packed from the moment you got off the elevator. Mort Zuckerman was talking to Amanda Burden. Charlie Rose was a foot away talking Jamie Goodale. Patricia Duff was talking to George Stephanopoulos and Alexandra Wentworth; Henry and Nancy Silverman, Alice Mayhew talking to Hannah Pakula, Peter Pringle, Peggy Siegal, Warren and Olivia Hoge, Jim and Kathy Hoge, John and Joan Jakobson, Robert Silvers, Susan Burden, the Rohatyns, Steve Ratner and Maureen White, the Brokaws, Paul Sargent, Editor of the WSJ, Carl and Barbaralee Diamonstein-Spielvogel, Steve and Cathy Graham, Liz and George Stevens, Judy Miller, Ina and Robert Caro, Lloyd Grove, Governor Jon Corzine and Sharon Elghanayan, and on and on."

Marcia Riklis, his second daughter (and third off-spring from his first marriage), has an equally enviable Park Avenue three-bedroom home with an appraised value in 2008 of $13.5 million. Her house in the Hamptons made news when she asked just shy of one million dollars for a 3-month stay at the sprawling 12-bedroom getaway overlooking the ocean and Shinnecock Bay.

And that's just the tip of the Riklis real estate personal property, since Meshulam Riklis, who just turned 90 on December 2nd is a father of five, a grandfather of 7, and a great-grandfather. This Riklis family empire extends to his sister and her children and relatives in Israel -- all of whom live like royalty. Their private real estate holdings are nothing compared to their portfolio of income producing real estate properties with an emphasis on shopping malls.

As noted earlier, Ted Arison gave up his U.S. citizenship and moved to Israel in 1990 to avoid U.S. taxes on his estate. Had he lived another 10 years he would have become exempt. However, he died in 1999 and missed the tax break. Meshulam Riklis moved to Israel at the same time as Arison and for the same reason.

He left the United States in 1990 and ten years later in 2000 at the age of 86 he married his third wife 58-year old Tali Sinai. She became one of the stars of "The Real Housewives of Tel Aviv"—a takeoff on the popularity of the franchise.

Meshulam Riklis died on January 25, 2019 at the age of 95. He was luckier than his friend Arison and avoided paying estate taxes having lived close to two decades in Israel after renouncing the U.S. citizenship which had made him a billionaire several times over.

An interesting and ironic tidbit is Ira Riklis's home security conglomerate consisting of the wholesale

C.O.P.S. Monitoring (which in typical Riklis style is a subsidiary of Lydia Monitoring, which belongs to Sutherland Capital, which in turn, is owned by Ira Riklis and its retail sister Safeguard Security which acquired and become known as AEG Security, which then acquired Matrix Security Group): nevertheless, it is the largest home security business in the United States, and it's initial funding came from Rapid American Corporation. It seems somewhat odd to think of any of these companies owned by Riklis offering Americans "home security" while from the very beginning he was ensnared in one of the largest personal injury lawsuits in history.

At the time Rapid-American filed for chapter 11 protection against the onslaught of asbestos related lawsuits the number of open cases was 275,000. No one knows the exact number of people who have asbestosis or mesothelioma or those who have died as a result of their exposure to asbestos. A fair estimate would be one million people, or more.

The bankruptcy files contain the following two statements:

"At this time, the addresses for each of the personal injury claimants are not available to Rapid, and gathering the individual addresses would require both a massive manual review of the files maintained by various past and present asbestos defense counsel across the nation and a time- consuming attempt to ensure that such information is still accurate (and if not, to obtain updated information).

"Historically, Rapid has maintained a bank account at JP Morgan Chase. Rapid utilizes preprinted checks, stationery, and other forms associated (the "Business Forms") with the JP Morgan Chase account. There is approximately $5,000 in the general bank account.

The Riklis's became billionaires several times over while the bank account for their main holding company was left with a mere $5,000. And, they got away with it.

Thirteen

Sam Giancana, whose real name was Salvatore, from whom Ira's father purchased the New York mansion at 15 East 75th Street was an Italian-American Mafia boss. He was a drug lord, a drug trafficker, an underworld kingpin, an extortionist, a pimp, a hitman, a contract killer, a racketeer, and mass murderer who was the boss of the powerful Chicago Outfit from 1957 until 1966.

He was a powerful and notorious mobster who mingled with Hollywood celebrities, famous actors, actresses, showgirls, sex symbols, models; as well as hobnobbing with judges, mayors, governors, senators, powerful politicians and Joseph Kennedy Sr (the father of John F. Kennedy). He had affairs with iconic sex symbols and supermodels like Marilyn Monroe, Jayne Mansfield, Sharon Tate and Angie Dickinson. He was engaged to Phyllis McGuire who was the lead vocalist in the 1950's hit trio the "McGuire Sisters". The couple had been introduced by Frank Sinatra. Sinatra had a habit of introducing beautiful women to his Senator friend, John F. Kennedy. After Phyllis became Giancana's girlfriend he introduced her to Kennedy who quickly seduced her.

Giancana was also involved in a CIA plot with fellow mob bosses Carlos Marcello and Santo Trafficante, Jr. to assassinate Cuban communist dictator Fidel Castro.

It is believed by the FBI and members of the United States government that the trio masterminded and ordered the assassination of President John F. Kennedy. They set up Lee Harvey Oswald as the fall guy and with the help of CIA snipers and dozens of mob assassins that kept an eye on Oswald to make sure it went according to plan. It is said they also had help from several corrupt FBI agents to make sure the assassination went smoothly.

Giancana built an $800 billion a year criminal empire and he had political influence and reach all over the world – transnationally. During his reign he was one of the wealthiest and most powerful people on the world. For over two decades he was a multi-billionaire at a time when millionaires were considered top of the game. His net worth was $30 billion.

The way he purchased the five-story mansion on East 75th Street (not far from where Leslie Wexner of The Limited and Victoria's Secret would purchase 9 East 71st Street for Jeffrey Epstein) was through the woman in his life. It is like using a "straw buyer". One can hide the true ownership of any property and a lot of the mobsters and wealthy men who were propped up by the same mob guys, like Ira's father, liked using their wives or girlfriends as the listed owner of various homes and apartments. This way they could avoid having anyone trace it back to them. It was also a way to launder dirty money. Only the girlfriends and the wives would know who owned what and where the money came from.

During the 1975 Church Committee hearings in the Senate that investigated the abuses of the CIA, it became known that they had recruited Giancana and other underworld figures to assassinate Fidel Castro. Giancana, at the time made the chilling statement, "The CIA and the Cosa Nostra were different sides of the same coin." Among the things that came to light were that Judith Eisner who was described as being "stunningly beautiful" was introduced to John F. Kennedy by Frank Sinatra in 1960 when he was still a Senator. Their relationship continued after he was elected President of the United States. She was simultaneously sleeping with Giancana, whom she also met through Sinatra. During this time she delivered communications to both men about Castro. In an odd twist, Giancana's daughter Antoinette, alleged her father was running a scam to pocket millions of CIA dollars.

On June 19, 1975, right before Sam Giancana was scheduled to appear before the Church Committee who was investigating ties between the CIA and the Cosa Nostra, Giancana was murdered. He was shot a total of 14 times—once in the back of his head, six times in his face, and seven shots in the neck. He had been in his basement kitchen frying sausage and peppers for his guest whom he knew, and who is suspected to have been of his murderers. There was no forced entry into his house.

At the time, the FBI were running a 24/7 surveillance on Giancana and would have been stationed right outside his home. On the night of his murder they were not there. Someone gave the order to pull them off duty so that the hitman could escape unseen. Rumors persisted that he was killed on orders of the CIA.

William Colby who was the Director of the CIA at the time said, "We had nothing to do with it."

Fourteen

The day I left "the business" began like any other. I only have 'regulars' and am seeing a well-known cartoonist, Ray (name changed), for one hour this afternoon.

"Hi," I whisper sweetly, swinging open the door.

"It's great to see you," he smiles broadly, with the warmth of someone's favorite uncle. "It's been a while…a long while." Ray's hand absentmindedly pushes back his silvery white crop of hair. He strides towards my bedroom carrying a parcel, and looks as if he's headed toward a podium to give a speech on illustrating.

I follow him, concentrating on his widow's peak. I have one too, and when I was a little girl, I heard an old wife's tale—if you have a widow's peak, you'll outlive your mate. I stare at his and the image of his wife springs to mind.

"About a month, you must have been busy to stay away so long. I've missed you," I coo. And as clients go, I really did. He's a nice man and a wonderful artist. I'm a great admirer.

"Before we start, I have a gift for you. It comes from here," he places his hand over his heart. "You're just a marvelous girl." His blue eyes twinkle mischievously. He offers me the package, and begins to shed his clothes. He is an older man and I always try not to stare at his wrinkly flesh. However, he is a famous artist and has a crush on me and so instead of declining the gift, I accept.

I begin to remove the plain brown wrapper as I sit on the bed next to him. I discover thin white sheets rolled tightly and held in place with a rubber band. Ever so gently, I push the rubber band off, careful not to damage the paper. There are three sheets in all, which I smooth out over my lap. I gasp as I absorb what he has drawn.

"I did them from memory, I usually like to work from a photo, but with you," Ray stops mid-stream; perhaps already sensing something isn't right.

Quickly I move from one to the next. I am naked in all three, with the exception of my ever-present high heels. The first shows me opening the front door with only Ray's large nose protruding into the apartment. The second shows me walking away, my ass bare for the world to see, and in the third, I am returning from the kitchen, carrying a glass of wine for him. My eyes are glued to the graceful, flourishing and bold circles, which form images of me. Suddenly, my mind is racing. How many of these are there? Has he been drawing me from the very start? What is meant as a gift feels like a trespass. Up to that moment I have been able to hold on to my pain. Even at my very lowest, I have been able to stop from slipping away. The woman in these pictures is a whore. No matter what I do, I will never live this down. Ray is saying something but I can't hear him. I hear myself thanking him. The fragments of who I have become are sometimes painfully evident. I offer an excuse about not feeling very well. It is the first time I break in front of a client.

He is astonished. Almost fearful. His eyes wide, his steady hands tremble as he gathers his clothes and within minutes disappears. I am beyond caring. I am alone with the sketches on white parchment and as I

143

examine them again and again I cannot bear it. The drawings which I'm aware are worth thousands and thousands of dollars, I destroy.   I tear the offending images, turning works of art into confetti, and desecrate them further by throwing handfuls of inch sized pieces down the incinerator where I hope they will burn. Along with my past.

Fifteen

Six months later I have found my way back to school and resumed my studies as an Art History major. I have even gotten a part time job as an administrative assistant for a bank owned company that buys and maintains airplanes.

It is a particularly cloudy October afternoon in 1986 and I sit cross-legged on my sofa in big slouchy socks, a pair of jeans and a baggy gray sweatshirt. About a dozen oversized books lay scattered beside me as I read and re-

read the passages I've outlined in yellow to prep for midterm exams.

I focus on an image of two figures. A man and woman are seated together in a French café. They appear to be in a catatonic state. At first glance they seem to be dressed appropriately until you realize they are not. There is a sense of carelessness in what they're wearing. Their clothes look as if they have been slept in, they are disheveled, and it is easy to imagine they may have that offensive smell of the homeless. The eyes of both figures elude mine. While the man looks to the right, the woman stares vacantly downward, her body is slouched, she is an empty vessel. A simple gust of wind would easily push her onto the table where her once youthful face would smash into the glass with the cloudy greenish poison.

The painting is Edgar Degas' L'Absinthe. She is lost to the wanderings of her mind. I cannot help but linger at the image because there is something that is as disconcerting as it is familiar. I recognize her sense of alienation. She doesn't belong to the world anymore. Although I do not drink, nor do I use drugs, I have become close friends with loneliness and isolation. And as I ponder this unsettling thought, the buzzer of my apartment rings loudly.

Not just one time, but constant. Someone's finger is stuck like glue to it and I am assaulted by the jarring noise. It fills up every corner of my small apartment and I can feel it vibrate in my body. Fear wells up inside me. I'm not expecting anyone and try to ignore it but it grows louder, more persistent. I sit quietly, close my book, and wait for the person to leave. I'm trapped.

After ten long minutes of trying to get past this and let whomever it is to tire themselves out, it continues. Anger takes over fear, and pushing my books aside, I make my way to the intercom to see what asshole is being such a pest.

"Who is it?" I bark sharply.

"It's me, Ira."

I let out an audible gasp and stand there confused. I am thrown off my center and quickly look around my apartment to remind myself that I am home and not in my work apartment. It doesn't even exist anymore.

My heart begins to race, and skip beats, and I can hear it against my chest. Thumpty thump. Thumpty thump. I wonder if maybe I heard incorrectly and so I ask again: "Who is it?"

"It's me Ira," he repeats.

I let go of the button and gasp for air trying to remember everything I ever told him. I know I never told him my real name. I never told him anything that would lead him here. But somehow this client, this Ira, this person, who is to me like every other man I met at a time in my life that I really just want to forget, this intruder has the audacity to be standing in my lobby with his finger on my buzzer and has crossed into my space.

My personal space. My life. My real life. A life he knows nothing about. A life he has no part in.

I'm reeling. How is it that Ira is standing in the vestibule of the small eyesore of a building I live in?

My apartment building is perhaps the ugliest on otherwise pretty tree lined street where families live in private town homes and well-maintained brownstones. It is over 100 years old and looks every bit its age. It has a drab gray exterior, and an unsightly stoop, with seven steep tilting steps. They are as narrow as they are high. There are odd cracks here and there with loose and missing pieces of concrete as if a giant had at one time placed one massive foot on the whole of the stairs leaving his footprint behind. They are tortuous to climb.

In years to come I will look back at that defining moment and will realize I did not think about Ira's own apartment, or apartments, as he later explained, having taken two enormously huge co-ops and merging them into a palatial home on ultra-glam Park Avenue, the most exclusive residential address in the world.

Ira lives in a spectacular limestone covered building oozing magical beauty in every detail. Designed by Warren and Wetmore—an architectural firm owned by Whitney Warren 1964-1943) and Charles Delevan

Wetmore (1866-1941) Their most famous collaboration was the construction of Grand Central Terminal in New York City. It is this level of craftsmanship that exists in the sought-after address well known among the elite for its spacious and unique layouts. Apartments with beautiful twisting wrought iron staircases, soaring 18-foot ceilings, original stone floors, all of which have over-sized windows overlooking Central Park and the Metropolitan Museum of Art.

His neighbors have names like Astor and Rockefeller; and Barbara Hutton and Samuel Kress. In 2007 *The New York Times* summed up the decadently beautiful building in an article aptly named, *"Where Sumptuous is no Exaggeration"*. The article describes Samuel Kress's penthouse apartment in exquisite detail, "It appears that almost all of the finishes in the apartment are original, or very lightly redone, from the 17th-century Venetian ceiling in the salon to the dreamy azure glaze on Mr. Kress's dressing-room cabinets to the original refrigerator, drainboards and other kitchen equipment…Samuel Kress gave great amounts of his collection to the Metropolitan Museum and the National Gallery of Art." The article ends with, "This apartment has seen more great art than any other space in the city." Kress made his fortune selling to poor people. He pioneered the five-and-dime stores, which because of their low price point, had a wider customer base than department stores.

Targeting the poor for profit has made many people exceedingly wealthy.

Park Avenue is the only location in all of New York where you will see flowers even on the coldest and most miserable days of the year. Where begonias, cherry trees, and tulips line the median that separates the traffic going North and South. Nothing ever looks bad or feels threatened in this small enclave of approximately twelve city blocks that make up the New York City neighborhood where only the very rich live behind heavily guarded doors.

The life of the high-class girl call who wasn't ever real and the real me are at odds with each other. One doesn't exist anymore and the one that is left doesn't know how to handle this sticky and quite unexpected situation. Somehow Ira has climbed the steep, broken and narrow steps of the building where I live and has pushed through the rules of blurring.

If I ever see a client or former client on the street, we know to ignore each other. No one ever acknowledges knowing the other person. It is a time-honored tradition and one that Ira has not only broken, but shattered.

I'm frozen and the flashbacks begin. I remember my other apartment, and while it was visually nicer than the place I call home, it was merely a workplace. A place where men would come and go. Literally. A stage for fantasies and the childish dreams of men who never want to grow up.

I take a deep breath and exhale slowly because my chest feels like it's caving in. I place my finger on the speak button.

"I'm busy, go away." My voice is stern and I hope he'll understand he's not welcome.

"It's taken me six months to find you, just give me, ahh, one minute," his disembodied voice seeps into my apartment.

"No!" My body begins to tremble with fear. Oh, please make him disappear I whisper quietly to no one. Please, please make him disappear.

"Just let me speak to you for a few minutes, please," he begs like it makes a difference.

"No! Give me your phone number. I'll call you in a few days." I lie, then because I cannot think I add, "I'm studying for midterms," and immediately after those words leave my lips, I want to reach out and take them back. That's too much information to give this non-person, this john, this intruder.

"No," he argues his voice is now louder, stronger. "Give me your number and promise to meet me for lunch at The Plaza on Thursday. Do that and I'll go away."

"Promise?"

"Promise," he echoes.

Like an idiot, because I can barely breathe let alone think, I give him my real phone number. Less than one minute later my phone rings.

"I couldn't wait till Thursday," he chirps smugly. In my mind's eye I can see him standing at the old phone booth on the corner of Broadway across the street.

"How did you find me?!" I demand.

As if losing his composure, he fires off a flurry of sentences. "I hired a retired police officer I know. I give a lot of money to their police functions. Dave is his name and I trust him to keep this quiet. I paid him $150,000 to find you for me. It took six months. I've missed you. I love you. See me please," his voice is softer than it was one minute ago. He almost sounds like a child pleading for the return of his favorite toy.

I'm too dumbfounded to say anything. I'm taken aback by the $150,000 figure. That is a lot of money. The whole thing is so invasive. I have been hunted down. And now my head does a backward somersault. How did he find me? How did find me? Oh my god, how did he find me?

I felt inherently violated. For some odd reason Rita Hayworth pops into my mind and I recall her famous quote: "Every man I knew went to bed with Gilda and woke up with me."

It was exactly how I felt. I wasn't the vamp he met when he paid for sex. I was just an ordinary girl.

What I will not know for years to come is that Ira has been spying on me. He already had my phone number. Asking me for it was just a ruse and I'm being followed wherever I go. Two days later on Thursday I meet him at The Plaza when it was still The Plaza before Donald Trump bought it as a trophy. "The Donald" as everyone knew him didn't mind overpaying because that is how money is laundered. At least this is how it was explained to me by Ira.

The dreaded Thursday is here and I spot him as I cross the street south on Fifth Avenue toward The Plaza hotel. He's standing, pacing really, in front of one of the side doors. My stomach is exploding with butterflies as before I know it I am standing in front of him. He grins broadly and he nods hello.

"Let's go inside," he instructs almost in a whisper.

Without saying a word I follow him to the Oak Room. He never orders lunch. Two men walk in behind us and sit immediately to our right, which I think is weird since the whole place is empty. Are they his bodyguards? Are they following him? Are they there to have a good look at me? Nothing about this feels right and I simply want to leave. And, then Ira gave me a good reason to do just that.

153

"I want to see you exclusively," he tells me in a monotone voice as though he's ordering a glass of water. "Just see me, no one else. I'll pay you."

"I'm not for sale! The girl you met and the girl I am are two different women. I'm not interested!" Flush with anger and completely insulted I storm out of the plush hotel with ornate carpeting and dozens of oversized crystal chandeliers.

I will not know when I ride my bike through Central Park in the following days, weeks and months to come and bump into Ira on his own bike that it was not coincidental. He is, in fact, spying on me. He has become my shadow, my stalker. I am his obsession.

One of his spies has told him I'm in the park so that he can zip on over and chat me up. He is priming me by making me feel he is becoming my friend. In later years I will learn the proper word is "grooming".

I will not know for years to come—even after I become his mistress of many years that my phones are tapped and every single move is being recorded for him. Someone else is writing my diary for the sole purpose of one man's folly. In time I will succumb. But for now, the man who one day will turn me into his sex slave is merely spying on me. One day I will understand I was never his "mistress" at all. One day I will realize I was his "sex-slave." It's a term that wasn't even known in the days of Ira and me.

Sixteen

It's Saturday and Ira insisted we go to his new office. It is somewhat of a relief and somewhat of a put off because I know he wants to show off and possibly even have sex to break in the new space. It's like I don't have any say in this game of his. It feels like I'm on a moving train and I don't even know who, if anyone, is behind the wheel. Or even where it's going. Is Ira behind the wheel? Is it me? Is it someone else? I am clueless and adrift somewhere in another dimension. It can't possibly be Ira because he's so clearly head-over-heels over me. However, I am free floating on the outskirts of his life. His office. His wife. His children. His business. His trips. I occupy a world that doesn't really exist.

"I want, ahhh, your opinion on how it's decorated," the elevator doors slide open on the 16th floor. He has already explained to me that his new space is just 5,000 square feet and by comparison to his former digs at Trump Tower it's small. He likes it because of its location and because he isn't at his father's beck and call. It's still on 57th Street which is familiar to him. One day in the future I will learn that in New York City 57th Street is the street of spies. Just on the other side after the East Side of Manhattan becomes the West Side, Israel's Mossad has an office under the guise of a travel company.

Ira stomps out of the elevator and makes a left. It's easy to see he feels comfortable on his own turf. His gait, which is usually slow, is faster and more aminated than usual. He's wearing a simple white shirt, grey slacks and a blue and yellow windbreaker. He even looks normal instead of the multi-billionaire he is. That's the thing about being really wealthy and not recognizable. We can walk on the streets without having anyone look at us and go inside any restaurant without being noticed.

We wander into the first room off to the left of the elevator.

"I love the conference table, but, ahhh, you tell me what you think?" His arms open up like the wings of a bat before he places his pudgy hand on the boardroom table. He presses close to me and I shove my hand behind my back slipping it in between his loin and my ass.

"Hey, not so close, I'm examining your space here," I bark. It takes everything I've got to maintain a tone of lightness in my voice when what I really want to is scream and run. All he thinks about is sex, sex, and sex. That is what I am. I am the embodiment of sex. Ira chuckles and steps back an inch. For the moment I've won a small reprieve.

The office has one large window overlooking the side street and the opposite side is sectioned off by a glass wall. My immediate thought is so that he can keep an eye on his staff while he is in here talking with the other men who run the world. A garish oversized oblong conference table sits squarely in the middle.

I re-absorb his question and wonder why he's even bothering to ask since it's clear his decorator has already finished her work. Even if I bothered to tell him I disliked his choice would it matter? I decide to pretend it's wonderful like I do with almost everything he does or says.

158

"It's very nice," I lie casually and strut around the enormous table and the important looking regal chairs surrounding it.

What I won't know for another four years when I read a *New York Times* article in 1991 is why he moved. It turns out his father, Meshulam Riklis, moved out of Donald Trump's building by skipping out on the rent. This puzzles me because I know his father has mountains of money and was, in fact, one of the world's wealthiest men. I would learn that wealthy people are also the cheapest people. They take and take and refuse to pay for things the way normal folk do. Donald Trump in turn, filed a lawsuit, which read, "Under cover of the night they [Meshulam Riklis and wife Pia] moved out of two lavishly appointed floors of the Trump Tower they had rented for $100,750 a month, leaving about $1 million in unpaid rent." The lawsuit also charged that: "Mr. Riklis and his wife surreptitiously moved a host of paintings and antiques from the 18th and 25th floors of the glitzy skyscraper."

Ira's office at Trump Tower was on the 18th floor while his father's office was on the 25th floor. Even before the move, I'd gotten tired of his relentless calls complaining about the fact that his father wanted to see him "upstairs". He griped constantly that he was terrified of his father's temper and had developed ulcers to prove it. He barely slept and always looked tired with dark rings under his eyes.

The New York Times described his father's office:

"The executive suites with views of Central Park that Mr. Riklis maintained for five years at Trump Tower had granite floors, silk damask and lacquered wood walls, French antiques, museum-quality ancient Jewish artifacts, and a full-sized kitchen. Among the decorations in the suites were Old Master paintings and a life-size nude portrait of Miss Zadora that hung near Mr. Riklis's desk."

Ira had moved out before his father made his getaway with his holding company Rapid American Corporation, McCrory Corporation and rest of the Riklis's myriad of diversified companies that included everything from clothing (Botany 500), to luggage (Samsonite), to Playtex (tampons, and even the division that made the Apollo 11 astronaut suits for Neil Armstrong and Buzz Aldrin), to a hotel in Las Vegas (The Riviera), and almost every type of company in between.

I am lost in thought and suddenly feel Ira's hand under my arm as he ushers me out and back into the hallway. He shows off the rest of the office and points out where his assistant, Jackie sits, where his sister's office is at the rear to the left, and then turns us around and takes me to his private office. It is at the opposite end of the hallway.

"And this is my office," he beams as we walk into a beautifully appointed room with a large oak desk, a sofa, and a couple of chairs that appear as if they belong in an art collection in a museum. There were no sounds from the whirlwind of traffic and people below. It was as quiet as if we were in the middle of a forest even though the window overlooked the side of the street where the cars and the trucks and the buses zip through.

As I make my way in I spot a large museum-sized painting on the wall to my left. It is a portrait of his wife and their two children.

I stop to absorb its grandeur. I've never seen a life size painting of a normal person. She is standing and I can see the slight resemblance to Mary Tyler Moore which Ira had already told me about a hundred times. The two children stand by her side.

"That was, ahhh, her tenth anniversary gift."

"Impressive." I nodded and tried not to sound annoyed. It's like my feelings didn't matter. I didn't matter. Only he mattered. As a woman I knew what the painting represented. She had her eyes on him in every part of his inner sanctum. From any spot in his office her cold eyes followed. For a moment I felt the coldness of her icy fingertips on my skin like those of a demon waiting for just the right moment to squeeze the life out of me and I got goosebumps. I shook it off just as Ira pulled back one of the two chairs across from his desk for me to sit on.

"Have a, ahhh, seat," he holds it firm until I am snugly on it then he skips around the desk and drops into a large swivel chair.

I can't help but to notice the accoutrements of wealth lined up on the edge of the desk: an early Wall Street ticker machine, a Lalique crystal paperweight, a solid gold Tiffany desk clock, a rare Faberge egg. Certainly not your grandmother's tchotchkes I silently marvel at the treasures before me.

"This is my grandfather's cash register," his beams with pride.

"It still works!" he adds enthusiastically as he rings up numbers and the drawer pops open. I immediately think about my grandfather on my father's side who was a shoemaker. While he died long before I was born there was a part of me that took pride in the fact that my grandfather knew how to make something by using his hands. I dared not ask Ira what his grandfather did to have such a magnificent cash register.

He takes his seat again and hands me a check made out to one of the corporations he had me create. While I made far less money than what I earned during my working days and while Ira kept me on a very tight financial lease, he did from time to time hand me a check that covered most of my expenses. Lingerie, clothes to wear on our trips, food, rent.

"Don't use your bank anymore," he instructs. "Use my bank. The family bank," he emphasized so that I would understand he was serious.

"Which bank?" The hoops he makes me jump for everything is exhausting.

On another occasion he will have me acquire an American Express card. And, he has me create corporations to hide me under. It doesn't occur to me for a long time that I am a business expense. Whatever he shells out for me he takes as a business expense.

"The Bank of New York. There's a branch on the Upper West Side not far from you. Go there. Only bank there from this moment on."

"Let me show you my safe." He opens the door to the left of his desk (on the same side of the office as the creepy life-sized portrait of his wife). It is the size of a studio apartment in Manhattan. I follow him inside into his private man-cave.

"Amazing, one would think this is just a small closet. What do you keep in here?"

He smiles and bends down opening the safe which is in the middle of the room. There is a chair next to it. I watch with disdain as he pulls out issues of Victoria's Secret magazine. Underneath them are all sorts of financial documents. Stock certificates, bearer bonds, cash, papers.

"These are beautiful," he tells me as he opens a Victoria's Secret catalog and shows me some of the almost naked women.

I am neither amused or surprised but I stay with him, cross my arms and dart him a look as if to say "what are you doing?"

"Before, ahhh, I met you, this got me very excited. Now, ahhh, only you excite me."

Images of Ira jerking off to Leslie Wexner's Victoria's Secret catalogs flood into my brain. I am reminded that sex is never far from his mind. I must be a walking sex sign for him. Like the porn-filled 42nd Street with flashing neon signs and seedy theatres with dozens of adult films. That is what I am to him. A real life sex doll that doesn't say no, is always perfectly made up and never has a headache.

"Ahhh, I like that you wear the Lejaby lingerie I helped you buy in San Francisco because Wexner's lingerie is cheap stuff. I didn't like the bras you wore. The straps, ahhh, have to be near your shoulders," he looks at me and takes a deep breathe. "Take your blouse off." I begin to unbutton my cotton top. His eyes are like daggers on my skin and I dare not move. His lower lip droops as I let my top fall off me.

Ira reaches for my hand as if he were Prince Charming and I am Cinderella. It's comical because he does this really sleazy thing in such a gallant manner. I place my hand in his and he walks us out slowly and towards the leather sofa that sits across from his desk. He plops down and unzips his pants. Suddenly he cups my face and plunges his tongue down my throat. I push him away and take my spot on the floor where I get on my knees in the spot between his legs.

While his wife watches us from the portrait, I take his erect penis into my mouth. My mouth and tongue know the rhythm and timing. I mentally go over the list of things I need to pick up at the supermarket. I need orange juice and milk. I calm the queasy feeling of doom I always have when I am with him and flick my tongue softly, slowly around his penis in exactly the way he has taught me.

SEVENTEEN

I will not know for many years to come that the Bank of New York was a money laundering vehicle for the men in Ira's circle: his father, their business partners, their friends. People he spoke about like Robert Maxwell, Leslie Wexner, Donald Trump, Bill and Hillary Clinton, Michael Milken, Leon Black, Ivan Boesky (another spy), and many others. The secretive cabal of wealthy men who I know run the world.

Edmond Safra owned the bank and came from a banking family. By the time he was 16 he began working alongside his father, Jacob, in the family business located in Beirut, Lebanon. There, they engaged in precious metals and foreign exchange. The family moved from Lebanon to Italy, then to Brazil, and ultimately to Geneva, opening up private banks and expanding their financial empire with wealthy clients from around the globe. In 1966, Edmond Safra founded the Republic National Bank of New York. It was the third largest bank behind Citigroup and Chase Manhattan.

One of Safra's best friends was Robert Maxwell, the newspaper baron from London. Maxwell used Safra's bank to funnel dirty money from Eastern Europe.

As far back as 1957, Edmond Safra had been named as a drug trafficker in a United States Bureau of Narcotics report. Even though the accusation led nowhere and was withdrawn for reasons that remain unknown, Safra's name was linked to drug, gold, and currency trafficking, money laundering and organized crimes. In 1995 *New York Magazine* wrote that Safra's bank was "known on the street" as the bank that would send an armored car to pick up large sums of cash from its secretive customers.

It is alleged Safra was involved in the Iran-Contra affair; that he had arranged for the murder of a "security

167

specialist" who discovered a link between him and the arms-for-hostages scandal; that he had double-crossed the Medellin cocaine cartel; that he was very close to mafia's kingpin Mayer Lansky; and that his bank had laundered the drug-trafficking profits of Panama's General Noriega.

Manuel Noriega (1934-2017) was a Panamanian politician and military officer who was the ruler of Panama from 1983 to 1989 He had ties to the United States intelligence agencies. Until he was removed from power in 1989 he was one of the CIA's most valued intelligence sources. Even though he was a conduit for illicit weapons, military equipment and dirty cash his handlers in the United States took no action because of his "usefulness" in their covert activities throughout Latin America.

On the morning of December 3, 2000 at 5am, Edmund Safra was awakened by his male nurse, Ted Maher, with the news that two masked men had broken in his home at 17 Avenue D'Ostende in Monaco. Maher had been stabbed three times. He was a former Green Beret who was Safra's right hand man. The Israeli army bodyguards, all Mossad, were supposed to be protecting him. However, Safra felt so safe in his penthouse apartment in Monaco that he kept his security team at La Leopolda - ten miles away. The assassins entered his home through one of the windows. His state-of-the-art security system had been breached and Safra retreated to his steel reinforced James Bond-style bathroom built like a bank vault. He took one of his nurses, 52-year-old Viviane Torrente, into the bathroom with him. And then the fire started. By the time the rescuers arrived two hours later, they found him and his nurse dead having suffocated by the fumes in the fire. A fire later found to have been deliberately lit. His body was blackened with soot, his skin had been completely incinerated. His eyes had popped out of his head like a ghoulish Walt Disney character.

~

I would one day come to know the names of people, organizations and large-scale infamous crimes. Among these Marc Rich, Bernie Cornfeld, Michael Milken, Leon Black, Robert Maxwell, Carl Lindner, Semion Mogilevich, Bank of Commerce and Credit (known as the Bank of Crooks and Criminals or BCCI), the Colombian Medellin drug cartel, the Pizza Connection, the French Connection, Jeffrey Epstein, Ghislaine Maxwell, Rafi Eitan, Adnan Khashoggi—but it was like a giant octopus with tentacles to the past, the present, the future and a cornucopia of people. It would give me a glimmer of understanding of how it connected to the Bank of New York and to Ira. But this took decades and one roadblock after another to overcome.

During all this time with a man who is a constant reminder of my previous life which I wanted more than anything to leave behind, he shares details about his own life like he's a neglected housewife. One with a new best friend with whom he can gossip with and share things he hasn't shared with anyone since maybe the beginning of his marriage. When he tells me that as a child he had an invisible friend named Theodore (after the President) I try not to act surprised. His father, he sniped, called him a sissy when he was brave enough to tell him.

Ira brags about how the family chauffeur taught him how to drive in their limousine as a teenager. He bemoans that he cannot wear "off-the-rack" clothing which makes it necessary to have everything handmade for him by Botany 500 – one of many family-owned businesses.

He tells me his best friends are Hollywood producer John Landis of the film "Animal House" with John Belushi fame and fashion mogul Kenneth "Kenny" Zimmerman of KENAR whose models include Naomi Campbell, Linda Evangelista and all the supermodels that also walk the runway for Victoria's Secret.

On a rare day when we do more than just have sex, we drive around in his red convertible Porsche with vanity plates: IDR. I find it vulgar and see it as a stark contrast to the respectable image he has been trying to convey.

When we're in another city I am embarrassed to sit in the white limousines he prefers and wonder why he isn't inclined to the more dignified and somber black car. Slowly, I discover his taste is similar to drug cartel mobster-style—gaudy, loud and obnoxious. He baffles me because he's full of contradictions. Is he a businessman? Is he a mobster? Is he in politics? Is he running the family's hedge fund? Is he a spy? I don't know who or what he is. The little I know is that the line between his father and the underworld mixed with the White House is blurry. They all fit into one odd-shaped box.

I discover Ira puts every single expense on his Rapid American Corporation credit card. He incentivizes his sales people (now selling home security systems because he had to make his $150,000.00 investment in me pay off), with small compact cars he gets at a discount or free.

When the family business named *The Riklis Family Corporation* decides to purchase E-II Holdings from American Brands he tells me his friends are buying the stock. It has yet to be publicly announced. I do not know he has told many other people and that he was in fact engaging in insider trading.

After the purchase of E-II Holdings which includes Elizabeth Arden he shows up with bottles of Narcisse Noir and Chloe asking me which of the two fragrances I prefer. I select the elegant old- world Narcisse Noir over the newer Karl Lagerfeld Chloe of 1975. Ira gives me a lifetime supply of the elegant tiny perfume in its classic black art deco box.

Black Friday, 1989

On Friday 13, 1989 I discover that Steve, the man who Ira has hired to sit on his seat in the Chicago Stock Exchange, is going to be fired because he didn't act fast enough when the United Airlines deal fell apart at the last minute creating a mini-crash of the stock market.

The crash became known as "Black Friday" and it was caused by the breakdown of a $6.75 billion leveraged buyout deal for UAL Corporation which was the parent company of United Airlines. The deal unraveled because the Association of Flight Attendants pulled out of the deal when management, during negotiations over the Employee Stock Ownership Plan that was designed to fund the buyout refused to agree to the terms.

Ira had invested what he felt was a "fortune" and instead of watching over the stock carefully on his own decided to spend the afternoon in bed with me. He must have anticipated a victory and not the complete collapse of the market.

He screams and shouts at Steve over the shoe-sized phone he carries with him at all times. His face is bright red with anger. I've never seen him this way. In my bedroom he is pacing back and forth, alternating between sitting on the bed with his hand on his forehead, and then back to pacing.

I listen to him complain about Steve after he hangs up on him. I then watch him spiral into a depression because of the money he's lost. I don't remind him of the monies he's made on deals that were illegal.

When everyone thinks him to be at the office he is in fact holed up in the History section of the New York Public Library. This is where he hides until he can collect himself and recoup the money he's lost. Ira begrudges the fact that he is "forced" to sell one of his Francis Bacon paintings for a mere million dollars. In my entire life I have been penny poor many times and I've had to sell my body and even now I am selling my body to him. Selling an object did not seem, to me, to be worthy of the anguish I witnessed during this part of the time we were together. Rich people, I discovered have a warped sense of what is worthy and what is not.

Pepe Le Pew

Among his favorite things to collect, aside from serious art, are Disney animation drawings called "cels" for celluloids. He likes the cartoon character Pepe Le Pew, a skunk who does not know how to take "no" for an answer, and who is obsessed with Penelope, a black cat who squeezed under a fence with wet white paint and who has a white stripe on her back. Penelope despises him because of his odor and his aggressiveness. On one our trips to San Francisco he buys me a Pepe Le Pew 'cel'.

It costs just over $700 while others in the store are worth thousands of dollars. Pepe Le Pew and Penelope epitomize who we are. I am a cat with white paint down my back in a world of delusional skunks.

EIGHTEEN

My father, I've been told, was a musician. He played the trumpet. I've heard wonderful stories about him. How he'd put on a tuxedo on those glorious nights he was able to get a paying gig.

How he'd go off to New Orleans; where, it is rumored amongst those who knew my father, he would meet up with the likes of Louis Armstrong, and the other jazz giants his generation, and play their sweet music together. Those were his favorite moments, I've been told.

As a toddler, when I'd just learned to walk, and still crawled on the floor at times, I'd find one of the many mouthpieces and stick one into my mouth. I've been told that I'd stubbornly refuse to let anyone snatch it away. I have no memory of this and regrettably don't remember much about him when I was a tiny girl. I knew I had a father and that he was always working.

There came a time in his life when his trumpet was taken away from him, as was his ability to lead a normal life.

The new apartment is big—many times the size of the other one. My sister, now almost 3, and I run back and forth through the long hallway with bedrooms on either side. In the background, we could hear mommy talking about daddy telling her friends, "He's crazy." I had no idea what crazy meant, or why we'd moved, or where he was.

Mom is fond of dressing us in matching dresses. I'm a whole year older than my sister and we don't look alike at all. But no matter how much I fuss, she always dresses us the same.

We're going to visit daddy today. I sit in the back seat of the car for what seems like a long, long ride. It bounces up and down and I feel sick to my stomach. I tell them I'm going to throw up. The car pulls over and I hop off and vomit on the side of the road.

After what feels like a really long time, the car pulls up in front of a very large ugly building. It's scary looking like an ugly castle with bars on every window. Daddy can't be in this place, I think silently to myself, and stop walking. I shiver and open my mouth wide so I can look at the cold air bubbles that pop up right in front of me. Beyond them I can see Mom and everyone walking further and further away from me. Getting smaller and smaller. Mom is carrying my little sister and I don't understand it at all because she can walk just fine. My older sister who is like my second mom is walking next to mom number one. Mommy's boyfriend Lou is walking between the two of them. I don't like Lou. I hate him.

They're so small in front of me now, they're going to disappear, and if they do what happens to me? So, I tap the pavement firmly with the tip of one shoe and my tiny legs begin to run as fast as they can until I catch up to them. They didn't seem to notice I was gone.

Awkwardly we all shuffle into the building with slow dragging feet like a giant injured octopus. My eyes are immediately glued to the walls where the paint color is different on the top than it is on the bottom. My head is just beneath the lighter color on top. The lower part is gray and dirty with brown smudges and black streaks. The stench of vomit and feces floods into my nostrils and I hear my little sister start to cry. She smells it too.

177

I follow my family into what looks like a big lunchroom. There are square tables and old worn chairs everywhere. I stare at a woman sitting in the corner of the large room with her blouse off and her arm held up over her head. Another woman who looks younger is shaving her underarm. I'm suddenly very afraid and want to go home. I almost start crying but stop myself because I'm a big girl.

We find an empty table and I spot daddy walking toward us. He smiles. I run to him. He scoops me up and hugs me and kisses me and suddenly I don't want to let go. "Daddy! Daddy! When are you coming home, Daddy?" He puts me down and takes a seat at the table.

His hands shake as he picks up the Pall Mall red cigarette box that looks like playing cards that mom brought him as a gift. He begins to puff on it, his eyes are shiny, he smiles and rocks back and forth. Back and forth. Back and forth. It's a little strange because he's sitting on a regular chair like the rest of us not a rocking chair. I look around and see other people rocking back and forth on their seats just like daddy.

After my mother packed us up and moved out of daddy's place and into a new apartment, things changed.

From that day on I am consumed with shame. It fills every pore in my body. It fills every part of my brain. My father is crazy. I can't tell anyone. I'll never tell anyone. I can't get the images of that horrible place out of my mind. For my entire school life whenever anyone asks me about my father I lie. "My father is dead," I tell them always wishing it's the last time someone asks. But, there's always the next grade and the next and someone is always asking.

"My father is dead!" I repeat in every grade in school until I am no longer in school and then I say it in real life. Saying this only deepens my shame.

Later in life, I will get to know my father for the last three years of his life. I will discover he was misdiagnosed. I will discover he had been one of the unsuspecting MK-Ultra patients experimented on without his consent. Thirty years after being admitted into an insane asylum as a ward of the State of New York floating from one mental hospital after another, he is released. No one can give him back the lost decades of his life, his golden gift for music or even his children who barely know him.

At around the same time, daddy was first admitted into one of the crazy hospitals, my older brother, who had also been sent away, and who may very well have been subjected to the same treatment as my father, committed suicide.

By now I was 6 years old and there always seemed to be another catastrophic event we had to survive. 1961 was the year my 21-year old brother hung himself while on vacation in the Caribbean. I remember him bringing home rope from the hardware store down the street. He built my sister and me a swing in the doorway of his bedroom.

We loved it. Johnny stood tall like a giant behind us pushing our backs gently as we took turns on the swing. "My turn! My turn!" We shouted over each other with the sort of exuberance only known to children. We weren't allowed to play with the other kids at the playground in school, and it was rare that mommy had time to take us to the park. And so, we really could not get enough of the gentle back and forth in the air. We laughed and giggled so hard until our cheeks hurt. Rocking back and forth and kicking our little legs up into the air.

We did not know for a long time he used the same rope to fashion a noose which he tied to a palm tree to commit suicide.

My mother never recovered from the death of her firstborn.

My sister and I were too young to understand the meaning of death – much less wrap our minds around the word "suicide". My mother simply told us "Johnny died". In the middle of a school day, years later, in a bathroom stall at the elementary school I attended I finally cried for him.

This was not our family's first experience with a traumatic event and it wasn't the last. Every member of my family had been sexually abused at some point during their childhood. My mother, my grandmother and all the children.

I would not, could not bring a child into this world.

My grandmother was born in Corsica—the same place as Napoleon Bonaparte—in, I believe 1900. This was a time when women and children had no rights. All were the property of the husband and the father. The father could abuse, rape and even kill the children or his wife and face no consequence.

By the time I was hunted down by a billionaire (part of the Jeffrey Epstein, Harvey Weinstein, Leslie Wexner, Ehud Barak, Leon Black, Michael Milken, Meyer Lansky group), I was the perfect selection. A lot of the grooming for me to become his sex slave had been done for him.

These powerful men, also part of a multi-generational lineage of rapists and pillagers know how to spot our broken wings. They swoop in and carry us off – when we're still in shock trying to survive the events that broke us to being with.

I would not know for many years into the future the how's or whys of what happened to me.

Nineteen

"My father wants to use my sperm so his new, ahhh, wife can have another, ahhh, baby," Ira's face is bright red and he's visibly upset. He's always upset at one thing or another and I always try to comfort him.

Hands over his head, eyes wild, he hisses, "You can't tell, ahhh, anyone."

"Who am I going to tell?" I'm surprised by the statement since he's never introduced me to anyone in his world.

"I can't do this. Have a baby and it's not mine?" He shakes his head, and moans and groans. I reach out taking one of his hands into mine.

"How do I say no to him? What am I going to do?"

"You're a grown man. You don't have to do everything he says." I try to offer him some comfort. To offer him solace. To sooth his pain. I forget he never soothed my own.

Abruptly he lets go of my hand, gets up and begins to undress. I quickly slip out of my dress that cost more than I can afford and climb back on the bed leaving my high heels on. His bright red Calvin Klein underwear and I are at eye level. I immediately know he is especially horny.

"My father has spent a lot of money, ahhh trying to turn his new wife into a singer, and now she, ahhh wants another baby. I didn't even know he'd had a vasectomy," he growls.

That he's never learned how to stand up to his father even now when he's making his own money surprises me.

I can see him sitting in Meshulam Riklis's office earlier before coming over. His father was known to boast that his wife, Pia Zadora, was 17 years old when they met but looked like she was 12. That statement alone was enough for anyone to know he was one of those men for whom women were reduced to trophies.

183

The furniture is in the French Empire style – a recreation the opulence found in Rome during the time of Julius Caesar. I recoiled in horror the day Ira told me his father sat on an armchair of gilded and ebonized wood that was made for Empress Josephine in 1895. The armrests, he'd explained, were elaborately carved to look like swans. She had a fondness for swans and they were found in almost all of her furniture. His father had acquired a lot of the furniture and art privately – so it had never been shown either in a museum or in an art gallery. Although Empress Josephine's regal arm chair was worth into the millions, Meshulam Riklis thought nothing of using it for his plump rear end as if it were a replaceable plastic chair. All this next to a life size portrait of a naked Pia Zadora next to this desk overlooking Central Park and Trump Tower.

"I hate that woman, ahhh, we went to a party at the, ahhh White House, and she ahhh wore a toga," Ira groaned beginning another attack on a woman I'd begun to feel sorry for.

However, I giggle appropriately which is what he expects, and it seems to relax him because he joins me and starts to laugh.

"Who else was at the party this time?" I ask. He flies off with his father regularly to Washington, D.C. to have their talks with Senator Joe Biden, who they hope to make President one day.

"Vanna White was there. She's not, ahhh, attractive in real life."

Politicians, businessmen, Hollywood celebrities and movie producers all pass through the revolving door of the White House. One time Ira tells me they gave a lift to Pope Paul II and Senator Joe Biden on one of his father's private planes from D.C. to New York. It doesn't make any sense to me at the time. Only as the years slip away will I ultimately understand how this strange assortment of people work under one umbrella.

He pushes me back against the pillows and pins both my arms up over my head. With the other he furiously flicks at my clitoris while staring into my face. His eyes are round almost like marbles. I fear they'll pop out and fall on me. It's incredibly painful.

"Stop, please stop," I plead.

Does he really think this is making me happy or is he getting off on hurting me?

Every time we have sex in this way it take me days to recover from the pain. I can't wear underwear or pants for several days and I'm pretty much home-bound. It's infuriating that he can't just treat me gently.

He picks up his clunky cell phone which is about three inches in depth with an adjustable antenna, and before dialing her, he whispers to me "I love you". Holding up one finger to his lips he motions for me to be quiet.

I ignore his declarations of love because I can't say these words back to him. I hate him.

And, I pretend not to listen as I hear her ask him what he prefers for dinner. It's incredibly funny and I stifle the urge to laugh. I don't understand why she has to ask him anything because I know they have a private full-time chef and she's not the one cooking. However, their little conversation goes on like this for a few more minutes as I watch him lie and then become annoyed. His words come out slower and deeper when he's upset. And by the time he utters the words "I love you" to his wife, he's plenty disturbed.

TWENTY

I like walking in the rain. With an umbrella over my head partly covering my face I can go anywhere and not hear the constant wolf-whistles, catcalling, or have random men chase me down the street asking for my name or my number. Being a woman in New York City is not easy. When it rains, I have the luxury of being invisible.

After walking for over one mile I recognized a diner and remembered that Mara lived on this block. I'd been to her apartment once before when we worked together at Warren's place a long time ago. I tilt my head backwards and look up to see if I could spot her air-conditioner. The last time I was here it was the only one that jutted out further than the rest which were neatly lined in a row. I saw hers and it was now sloping even further off the ledge.

On an impulse, I walked to the front door of the old building and pushed open the front door. The lock was gone and in its place was a hole where the lock had been. I peered at the mailboxes to see if her name was still on it and to remind myself of her apartment number. Mara Dobbs. Sixth floor. I'm so happy. She's still here. I walk back out into the rain and buzz her.

"Who is it?" She shrieks.

"It's Kirby!"

"Wow, come on up!"

She buzzes me in even though the front door is broken and I've already been inside.

I wait for the elevator which appears to be out of order and then climb the steps up to the sixth floor. I glance up and see her standing by the rail smiling and waving at me.

"It's so good to see you! Sorry about the elevator. It's been like that for a few days," she shouts.

As I take the last couple of steps I see an overweight woman with dark circles under her eyes and disheveled hair.

"Hi, nice to meet you. Is Mara home? I knew her a long time ago."

"Silly, it's me!" the overweight woman said, giggling and hugging me.

I am stunned and saddened to see her like this but I hug her back and pretend I didn't notice the change in her. I recall she is only five years older than me but looks maybe twenty years older and is at least 40 pounds heavier.

"Come on inside. The place is a little messy," she graciously allows me into her apartment and I leave the wet umbrella outside.

The place was an absolute disaster. It looked almost as bad as Mara did and I suddenly felt a pang of sorrow. I began to tear up and seeing me tear up she immediately teared up too.

"Hey, come sit down, let's not cry. We've got so much to catch up on. You look so pretty."

I followed her to the sofa and as soon as I sat down I could smell the liquor on her.

"Thank you, Mara. It's really nice to see you. It feels like a lifetime ago."

"You have no idea how crazy Warren got when you left and took his best clients with you! It was great to watch him have a meltdown!" She pounded on her chubby legs and crackled hysterically.

"I didn't care, Mara. I needed to get out of that place. I wasn't going to keep giving him half the money I earned. No way. Plus, the place was a dive." I said and began to relax.

"Do you want a drink?" She reached out and grabbed a half empty bottle of Vodka topping off her glass.

"I don't drink, remember?"

"You still don't drink? Amazing. But then you were always amazing. I wish I'd left with you. You were always so smart."

I wanted to grab her hands and tell her to stop drinking. To stop doing whatever it was she was doing to herself. It was painful to see the once regal looking showgirl look like an old woman on the verge of homelessness.

"Tell me, did cheap Ronnie pay your new rate when you took him with you?" she asked.

"As a matter of fact, he did. And then I raised it again," I replied with a giggle and a shrug.

"He was always such a cheap bastard. I remember he tried to con me once. Leave without paying. That's a hoot. I mean, pussy is pussy. And he paid more for you. That's so funny!"

"I guess. I stopped working a while ago."

"Really?"

"Yes, I went back to school and then I met a guy, and…"

"Oh, that's so good to hear. I'm so happy for you."

I didn't have the heart to tell her what really happened to me.

"Your turn. What's going on? Are you still at Warren's place?"

"Oh no. I left a few months after you did. I was raped and I had to stop." The smile on her face disappeared.

"What happened?"

She took a long gulp and then her words tumbled out slowly. "Well, Warren decided to expand and so he took the apartment across the way. There was this one guy one day that stopped by. It was my turn. He wasn't a regular. Anyway, like an idiot I want to try out the new place. So, the guy comes in, takes off his clothes and all the while, you know, I think I am being careful. I don't know if he's a cop of something," she pauses.

I lean forward and suddenly I realize she's in pain.

"He raped me."

"What do you mean?" Being in the business was a series of rapes. Nothing more than this. It is that brutal. There is no lovemaking. There are no nice guys. It's just one rape after the other.

"Well, after he had taken off his clothes, he tells me it's my turn and there was no money on the table, you know. I told him I would leave until everything had been settled and come back in a few minutes. He began yelling at me. Told me I was a whore and then he grabbed my arm and said he didn't have any money. He told me that if I didn't want my throat slashed then I should shut up and spread my legs. I tried to fight him. I mean I didn't want to fuck some asshole for free! But, you know, he was big. and he pinned me down," she paused and drank a little more. "Had I been at the other apartment I would have screamed for help, but I was at the new place and I couldn't."

I reached out and took her hand. "I'm so sorry."

"I was lucky though. Once he was finished, he left. He even thanked me." She added and stretched out her arm showing me a scar. "He left this though from his pocket knife."

"Oh, my goodness, I can't believe this." I knew I had taken too many chances when I was working all by myself. It's not like I didn't escape or had yet to escape without scars. Mine weren't as visible as the one on her arm.

"I was pretty shaken up for a while. I quit right after, though. I just couldn't do it anymore. I can't even have a boyfriend. It just turned me off to all men. I barely tolerate the old man who pays my bills. I have a girlfriend now and let me tell you women are even more evil than men are!"

All this was startling to hear. It made me feel like maybe I didn't have any real problems. Maybe being a sex toy for one man who didn't beat me wasn't a bad thing.

I needed to get out of here. I was suddenly fearful that maybe I was looking into my future. No way. No way. No way.

"Mara, I was on my way to an appointment. I'll come back another day," I stood before she could convince me to stay.

She grabbed a piece of paper and scribbled her phone number on it. "Let's stay in touch, Kirby."

Mara began to sob again.

"Are you okay? It's going to be okay." I try to soothe her, but the truth is she's far from being normal. She somehow slipped through the invisible crack where many girl like Mara disappear. The place from where there is truly no turning back.

"Yeah, I'm fine. Don't you worry about me. Go on. We'll talk soon." She patted her tears dry and put on her stern face.

Feeling a tinge of guilt, I hugged her and opened the door. I made a run for stairs and as I landed on the third floor, I heard her yell out my name again.

"Hey, Kirby! Kirby!"

"What?" I turned and looked up.

"Always remember," she said, her voice now slurred. "Never cast your pearls to swine!" She then slammed the door and disappeared.

I continued running and got myself out of the old tenement building and back into the pouring rain. The rain drops hit my face like ice pellets reminding me that what stood between me and becoming like Mara was a razor thin line. I pushed the terrifying thought away and walked as far away as I could from the apartment building. To calm myself down I tried focusing on her last words. Truth is, it would be years before I understood her sage advice.

TWENTY-ONE

Ira devours my life like Wile E. Coyote chasing the Road Runner. Few people know the coyote is based on Mark Twain's book 'Roughing It'. Twain describes the coyote as "a living, breathing allegory of *Want*. He is always hungry."

I fear I will tire out and fall apart at any moment. I live in uncertainty. Unhinged. I am tethered to nothing real. There are so many things I have had to do and so many hoops I have to jump through to accommodate his unwanted presence in my life. I had to stop taking classes because I need to be ever ready. To accompany him on his business trips; to entertain him in my apartment—which means lingerie and sex; to spend endless time on the phone with him multiple times every day listening to him complain about the woes of being rich. I exist only as a reflection of who he wants me to be.

My sleep is abruptly interrupted by the shrieking sound of the phone. The clock next to my bed tells me it's 7 a.m., and startled, I climb off. By the time I stumble into the livingroom to answer it, I feel the pangs of a headache.

"Uhhhh, hello?" I mumble my head in the palm of my hand.

"Join me for a, ahhh, short trip to San Francisco." Ira's voice is crisp and energized.

"When?" I yawn loudly unable to suppress my exhaustion. I straighten up because every time he's on the other end of the phone I feel he can see me.

'Today. I'll send a car for you and we'll met at the airport."

"Why today?" I moan and try to think of a reason why I can't go.

"Because my wife is out of town and it's easier. I'll call and let her know something's come up and I have to go to the coast. The nanny will take care of the girls. How about it?"

Because my head is beginning to throb, I agree. It's easier than telling him I don't want to go and have to counter his protestations.

"Atta girl! I'll call you in an hour and give you the details. Meanwhile I'll book my flight."

While I am busy packing, Ira rings again. He instructs me that a driver in a limousine will be stopping by my place at 10:30 a.m. and that our flight will be departing at noon from JFK.

"I'll meet you at the, ahhh, gate," he says in a self-congratulatory tone.

My relationship with Ira, or my servitude to him, is based on one thing: lies. He lies to the people in his life and I keep the people in my life out of my way. I can't tell anyone about him and he can't tell anyone about me, except for his accomplices like Dave who found me for him and who is raking in the big bucks. I am reduced to being a shadow and a perpetual prisoner. While I once had pin money, I no longer have even this because he keeps me on a very thin need-to-have allowance. Enough to paya my bills, but never enough to say goodbye.

As soon as I bounce down the front steps of the building, the driver, parked right next to a fire hydrant lumbers out of the black stretch limousine. We nod silently. I have learned by now how to cue the drivers before stepping into a car. I want no talking. He takes my bags, opens the back door, places the bags into the trunk and then slides into the driver's seat. I settle comfortably into the plush leather seat and press the button. The glass petition between the driver and myself slowly slides shut. He starts the car and in less than two minutes, we've turned left on Broadway, and are on our way to the airport.

I usually hate the 45-minute ride in a regular taxi with what is usually an inquisitive chain-smoking cabbie, torn plastic seats, and rear windows that never fully close. The only other time Ira got me a limousine all to myself was last year, in 1988, when my father died.

Out of nowhere, on that horrible morning as I dressed for my father's wake and funeral, Ira arrived unannounced at my apartment. He insisted I take what he called "the car". It was a nightmare. All I kept thinking as he talked and talked was that from this moment until the day I died whenever I remembered my father I would see Ira's face instead.

It would take decades before I realized the driver was a hired spy. Hired to find out about my family so that he could punish me by hurting them when the time came.

But on this day, on my way to the airport, I don't know this. Instead I try to find comfort in menial things like making sure my hair won't be a mess and my clothes won't reek of cigarette smoke—because despite the fact the limousine seems clean I can smell stale cigarettes as the stench permeates through my nostrils.

Ira and I have been to San Francisco before and we've already taken a couple of trips to Washington, DC, to North Carolina, and other places. One time, when we were supposed to take different flights and I made it to the airport late I grabbed the next flight out. To my shock I discovered, while boarding with the other first class passengers, that Ira and his family were just ahead of me. He looked straight into my eyes and then quickly looked away. I guess, he too, was surprised. However, I've always wondered how his wife didn't notice. The seating was even more of a disaster. I sat in the middle aisle and he was to my immediate left. His wife on the other side in the window seat. Behind them sat their two young daughters. It was a long six hour flight to the West Coast. The man on my right made a couple of passes at me. I tried to simply ignore him. I felt like I was on center stage and everyone was staring at me. If it was uncomfortable for me, it was just the opposite for Ira because the first thing he did after we respectively checked into our different hotels was to call and stop by for a quickie sex refill.

I can see him in my mind's eye now running out of his car and buying condoms. This is how he usually does it. He'll have the driver stop at a pharmacy and buy three boxes of Fourex lambskin condoms, the kind that comes three to a box. If I'm with him, I'll pick up hairspray or some other thing I've forgotten. Once when I handed him a small bottle of Aqua Net at the cashier, he told me he made twenty-five cents on every bottle sold. Faberge was one of his family's many holdings. He'd told me it had been a trophy buy for his father, Meshulam Riklis. I learned about how wealthy men bought companies just to add prestige to their reputations.

What Ira didn't tell me and what I would discover years later was that Faberge was being sued at exactly the same time of our trip for permanently injuring a minor. The company had secretly changed one of the ingredients, never informing the public because of the increased danger of the product.

On April 3, 1989, Alison Nowak, 14, tried to spray her hair with a newly-purchased aerosol can of Aqua Net. The spray valve would not work properly. Alison decided to cut open the can with a can opener which she had done before with the less flammable ingredient. She thought she could then pour the contents into an empty pump bottle of Aqua Net which had a working spray mechanism. Alison was standing in the kitchen near a gas stove when she punctured the can. A cloud of hair spray gushed from the can and the stove's pilot light ignited the spray into a ball of flame. Alison suffered severe, permanently disfiguring burns over 20% of her body.

Or that one of his best friend's client, Michael Jackson, who worked with John Landis on his 1983 music video "Thriller" where Jackson dances with a horde of zombies also suffered burns as a result of using Faberge's Aqua Net hairspray. On January 27, 1984 the pop star was in the middle of filming a commercial for Pepsi singing his hit "Billie Jean" when a pyrotechnic accident caused his hair to catch on fire. In reality, it was the Faberge hairspray that accelerated his burn.

≈

The limousine glides smoothly into the American Airlines terminal and I immediately spot Ira pacing back and forth next to the oversized revolving doors. The driver steps out into the sun and opens the door for me. I am wearing a navy-blue pin striped pant suit with no blouse and no bra under the jacket. The belt around my waist cinches the jacket closed and matches the creamy brown sling back pumps that are not practical and surely not meant for traveling. He hands me my overstuffed

Louis Vuitton carry-on bags and tells me the trip has been paid for.

I sense everyone's eyes on me as I begin to walk towards Ira who has stopped pacing and has seen me. My heels make a clickity clack sound against the sidewalk as I try to run-walk to him.

"Hi," I whisper almost out of breath as he reaches to hug and kiss me. "I thought maybe I was late," I add.

His face is bright like a Christmas tree and he smiles in a way that was is much more relaxed than he's been in a while.

"Hi," he says softly. "So happy you, ahhh, got here. I was hoping I, ahhh, wouldn't get stood up." He ushers me into the building and once we're in front of the reservations clerk, he orders a one first class ticket for the noon flight to San Francisco. Peeling off hundred dollar bills he places $2600 on counter. The clerk hands me the newly printed ticket.

"Where's your ticket?" I ask him.

"In my pocket," he replied, "I, ahhh, bought it earlier."

We check into the Fairmont on Nob Hill. It's an old hotel with old world elegance named after a notorious philanderer James Graham Fair whose wife divorced him in 1883. Fair had made his fortune quickly and promptly used his wealthy to secure a seat in the U.S.

Senate. He was known as "Slippery Jim" for his mean-spirited and vindictive ways.

I stand several feet away almost against the wall while Ira checks us into the hotel. My skin burns when the eyes of the men with their ordinary looking wives give me a once over on their way to the elevators. They all must know why I am here—of this I am sure.

Ira drops his briefcase and small travel bag next to the door to our room.

"I'm going to get this, ahhh, right, ahhh this time," he says and takes my bags placing them next to his.

"What are you doing?"

"I'm going to carry, you, ahhh, over the threshold." He scoops me up into his arms and grunts loudly.

"Be careful!" I protest.

"I've got you," he pushes the door open with his foot and carries me over the threshold like we're a newly married couple. He then drops me on the bed and his face shows beads of sweat.

He gets our bags, throws them into the corner and jumps on the bed.

"Come here you," he reaches for me and sticks his tongue deep into my mouth.

"I'm hungry," I say hoping to postpone the encounter.

"Me too! How about, I ahhh, take you to a restaurant I like and then we can, ahhh, do a little, ahhh, shopping?"

"Sounds great!" I bounce off the bed and head for the bathroom to reapply my lipstick.

Hand-in-hand we walk into Neiman Marcus after a quick but delicious mini-lunch. Ira pauses in front of the Elizabeth Arden display.

"I was just at the New York salon the other day for a facial," I begin as he drags me around looking at the display items. "You really ought to tell your father he has to train the staff better. They're rude."

"They're rude to me, too and I, ahh, ahh, own it," he retorts with a grin.

I sincerely believed I was providing him with important inside information as a customer of their newly acquired Elizabeth Arden. In 1986 his father, Meshulam Riklis, acquired E-II holdings which owns Elizabeth Arden from Eli Lilly & Company for $725 million.

Like everything else the Riklis's owned it was purchased via on corporate umbrella that disguised the real owners. In this case they used Faberge to buy E-II holdings.

In New York, I'd gone to the Fifth Avenue iconic store with the well-known bright red door and had gotten extravagant facial. Once I gave myself the luxury of a body wrap. They wrapped me up like a mummy in hospital with gauze as I lay down on a small table in one of their treatment rooms. Precisely one hour later the technician walked in and peeled the gauze off me. She handed me a towel to wrap around my naked body and asked me to follow her. I was escorted to a large open area with drain holes like a giant shower. The towel was pulled off me and a heavy-set woman with a water hose pointed in my direction turned it on. I almost screamed as cold water pounded my skin over and over again. Then in a Russian accent she said, "This is the same treatment we give Raquel Welsch."

Ira and I only hold hands in other cities and when he's done poking around the Elizabeth Arden counter he leads me onto the escalator except he doesn't let go of my hand.

"Hey, let me go or I'll fall," I say playfully.

"I'll never let you go."

I pull myself loose from his grip and then he wraps both hands around my waist from behind. As we step off the escalator a woman with bright red lipstick immediately smiles at us.

"May I be of help?" An older woman with a Spanish accent wearing a plum-colored suit and lots of fake jewelry asks before we've even stepped off the escalator on the second floor. It was clear to me she spotted us and smelled a heavy spender. Across her face is a fake smile that saleswomen use when they spot a wealthy man with a beautiful woman who is not his wife. By now I can tell when they know. The film *Pretty Woman* with Richard Gere as the corporate raider and Julia Roberts as the hooker is a couple of years away. When the movie is released in 1990 and I watched it for the first time I was immediately transported back to this day and this moment.

"Ahhh, yes, my friend here is looking for, ahhh, a few things. Perhaps you might, ahhh, have something she would like," he replies and I immediately want to elbow him because I prefer to shop on my own.

"My name is Cecelia," the smile on her face looks even wider now. "Come on dear, I've got some wonderful dresses that would look marvelous on you."

In less than 20 minutes Cecelia cradled half a dozen outfits over her arms.

"Come on," she said with an acquired haughtiness as she walked towards the dressing room. "I'll put these in here and you can try them on."

The dressing room is the size of a studio apartment in New York. An ornate replica of a Regency sofa is pushed up against the wall. Ira promptly plops himself down. I watch with horror as Cecelia hangs the outfits on the various hooks and then my eye catches Ira grinning in anticipation.

She shuts the door behind her and my reflection bounces back from the three different angled mirrors. I see myself three times and I see him four times.

"Are you here to watch me strip?" I ask sarcastically seriously hoping he'll leave me alone for a few minutes.

"You betcha." The lascivious grin is glued to his face as he rests his left elbow against the arm of the sofa and cocks his head to one side.

There's only one way out of this. Plow through it like walking against the wind. By now, I do this a lot. I stay in character.

"Okay. I accept the challenge. Hold on to your seat!"

I begin to bump and grind to the music filtering into the dressing room. Slowly, I unbutton the short tight blouse I'd changed into before we left the hotel and fling it at him.

I turn around and slowly unzip my skirt, then I face him again and slip it off. I throw this at him too and he catches it. He's holds it with both hands as he leans forward with wide eyes and a silly grin.

Down to only a bra, a skimpy pair of panties and my high heels I lower myself down to him and he takes one of my nipples into his mouth.

"That's all for now," I push him away.

"You little tease."

"I have things to try on."

But with every outfit I toy with him until Cecelia knocks on the door.

"Is everything okay in there?"

"Yes, ahhh, everything is fine," Ira answers.

He's annoyed by the interruption.

"Is there anything you don't like or maybe you need another size?"

"No, no, everything is, ahhh, fine," he yells. "We're taking it all!"

Once the plane lands at JFK airport, he kisses me lightly on the lips and whispers "Goodbye." Everyone stands the second the plane pulls into the gate even though the door won't open for another 10 minutes. Ira and I stand too. Except now it's like we're strangers. He instructs me, as he always does, to leave the plane first, without looking back, to get into a cab and go straight to my apartment. It's over. I'm free. At least for today.

TWENTY-TWO

1990

Ira now owned Dave's security company named Alarm One—or rather he made himself a partner. He always referred to Dave as "the former police captain who I paid $150,000 to find you for me." The company is small two-man business run by Dave and his brother-in-law. They have an office in New Jersey along with a phone number that begins with 800 and spells out name of their company that I think is clever.

Ira and I speak about it often. We compare it to being a gold mine. And it turns out to be just that. One day in the near future it will become the largest wholesale supplier of home security services in the world.

Dave, his new business partner, had little choice in the matter. Ira liked to snicker about how Dave had gotten married for the second time to a much younger girl from Colombia who was having a blast spending his money faster than he could earn it. All of which gave Ira the leeway he needed to take over Dave's retirement gig.

We've just finished having sex and he is stretched out on my bed. The sun has lowered since we stumbled into it earlier in the afternoon. He has finally stopped the annoying habit of asking me if I have people hidden in the closet filming us in bed. My small bedroom is darker and the lightning gives it an exotic quality making if feel as if we're lost somewhere on vacation.

He's holding me with both arms tight against him and I snuggle deep against him. It is what we do after every sexual encounter. I pretend to be happy. He pretends to love me. It is a cycle I don't know how to break out of. I can no longer see the outside world.

Even after the painful sex I let him cuddle me as if nothing is wrong. We're naked and his chin bobs up and down on my head as he speaks.

"I made him an offer he couldn't refuse…" he starts and pauses and I know he wants me to say something about his Godfather movie reference, but I don't. I say nothing during his rehearsed pause because I hate him for following me into my real life.

He never tires of telling me how difficult and expensive it was to find me. "After all, I had to make sure Dave would never talk about what he'd done for me by finding you. The business turns out to be a cash cow and I've already made my money back and am expanding it everywhere. I owe you a finder's fee."

I should have pushed for that "finder's fee" but I didn't. I really never wanted to feel like he was paying for me. At some point, however, Ira allowed me to open up a small store. He gave me zero advice but he certainly had plans for how he was going to keep tabs on me.

While I was in the middle of renovating the tiny commercial space for my American folk-art store in New York City, Ira had Dave and his brother-in-law come over and install a security system. I didn't understand it because he'd already told me not to have more than $15,000 in stock at any given time. And, I'd already bought a wrought iron door for the front door and thought it had remedied my security issues.

Ira was adamant about having an alarm system installed. He told me to tell the contractors renovating my new store to take the day off. He was going to have Dave and his brother-in-law stop by and do the installation themselves.

On a gray and rainy Saturday afternoon Ira and I met at the store and were joined by his two business partners who each shook my hand politely. I sensed they were uncomfortable since they both diverted their eyes away from me during the awkward handshaking ritual.

It was weird to see the big bosses of what was now a large company in my tiny hole in the wall store instead of one of their professional installers. Ira always bragged about how many new salesmen they'd recruited. Most were former police officers or detectives.

Dave gave me no outward sign of recognizing me. Not even a quick chit-chat about finding me for Ira. I had been hoping to hear his side of the story, but he said almost nothing. Both men looked away every time I glanced their way. Had it not been for the "hellos" at the front door, I would have thought they were deaf, blind and mute.

Ira made up for their silence and was unusually cheerful. In a voice louder than his usual tone he began to instruct them on what needed to be done.

I tip toe up the stairs into my small office. It feels like I am an intruder in my own store.

"No exposed wires anywhere!" I overhear Ira bark at them sharply, time and time again, as they spent the afternoon in the shop with all sorts of wires and equipment. It was the only time I'd ever heard him be curt with anyone. At least in person because he could be just as stern when he was on the phone with someone who wasn't doing what he wanted them to do.

A couple of hours later they're done and Ira asks me to come downstairs and enter a couple of codes into the newly installed gray box next to the front door. He suggests I punch in our birthdays suggesting these are good because I won't forget them.

Ira never had Dave and his brother in law do the same for my apartment and even on that day I remember thinking how odd it all was. Three wealthy men playing around in my tiny store for hours hiding wires. For what they all claimed was being done for my "protection".

Years later I would discover that professional alarm installers instruct their customers not to use personal information such as family names, pet names, social security numbers or birthdays as security codes.

I have long suspected in all these many years later, that on the dark and dreary Saturday afternoon when Ira and his partners were installing a security system in my tiny store, they were instead installing an eavesdropping system. I also believe my phones were bugged at the same time.

Using our birthdays as the entry code gave him and his men the ability to go into my store for upgrades like installing hidden cameras whenever they wanted to and I'd be none the wiser.

It would take decades until the pieces of everything done behind my back fit. By the time the random bits of information settled into a pattern and made a wee bit of sense my store would be long gone.

TWENTY-THREE

1991

The discomfort of the oppressive heat oozing out of the radiator on this boiling June night intensifies the unfathomable images dancing round and round in my head. It's just a few minutes past 11 p.m. on a Saturday night, and with two stores to tend to along with the recent pile of worries Jesse has dragged into my life—prompting me to get a restraining order against him—I'm beyond drained.

215

Sleep is eluding me. Teasing me. It has played this wicked game with me since the day Ira Riklis crossed over into the untouched part of my normal self. But what really happened after his hostile takeover of me is I have become his sex slave. I am stuck inside an invisible bubble thwarted by this man-boy's obsessive lust, who sees me as body parts: ass, breasts, legs, hair, pussy.

The thin white sheet on my naked body feels like a goose down comforter and I push it off. It lies flat the way wind will suddenly disappear out of a billowing sheet so that it is limp beside me. Turning on my side with my hair falling over my face I remember it was Chris who brought Jesse to me.

The Gulf War has had economic ramifications on small businesses in New York. I sell hand-made crafts from artisans throughout the United States in a tiny store on the less trendy Columbus Avenue. Although I have celebrities like Bruce Willis and Barbara Streisand that come in, primarily these are impulse buys for the regular consumer. My only competitor is the Museum of American Folk Art who make their money in donations.

I don't want to ask Ira for money. First and foremost, I want to prove to myself that I can take care of myself in a normal way. Secondly, if I were to ask him for anything, he would make it such a complicated set of hoops, each requiring my having to see him, or speak with him face to face, when I know it's just another carrot on stick game he plays to get near me. To touch me, to control me, to fuck me. To squat down between my legs in front of my pussy, with drooling lips, while rubbing my clitoris raw. I can't play his game anymore.

With two stores and two apartments and four employees, I have to find ways to save money, I figure I can do this by giving up the nicer of my two apartments, and move back into the smaller one which I use as storage for the stores.

Moving my books is the problem. They fit easily into the wall-to-wall bookcase in my nice apartment but there really isn't any room for them at my smaller place. I can fix this by building a bookcase that resembles the one I have. It's a simple solution to a big problem.

I spend a couple of days calling about a dozen carpenters while perched in my office that sits in a small loft above my Columbus Avenue store. I gather quotes from all of them. And just as I have decided on which one to hire a heavyset blond man in his 30's walks into my store, unannounced and uninvited.

"Hi, my name is Chris, I just opened the hardware store around the corner," he gestures with his arm extending his plump hand.

"Nice to meet you." I slip my hand into his extended one, but his grip is so tight it's almost painful, so I pull away quickly.

"Yeah, I just retired from the police force and, you know…" he can't seem to stand still, shifting his weight from one foot to the other. "I, uhm, decided to open up a hardware store."

His hardware store is around the corner from my shop with just the corner deli separating the two. The rear of my store and a small portion of his shop share a wall.

"Aren't you a little young to be retired, Chris?"

He looks down at his feet, shuffles some more, and then he slowly raises his head to look at me. "I got hurt on the job so I retired. I don't want to keep you, but I just thought I'd stop by and let you know that if you need anything. Anything at all. Like, for example, if you need something to be built…"

"Yes! Yes!" I exclaim with the sort of excitement I haven't felt in a long time. "I need a bookcase built in my apartment. Is that something you do?"

"Absolutely can do!" His eyes perk up and he smiles. "Hey, I'll have one of my guys, uhm, his name is Jessie, out to your apartment later today."

"Wait a minute, how much is this going to cost me?"

"Three hundred dollars," he deadpans.

Everyone else I had spoken to quoted me a price that was at least three times what he just offered. I agree on the spot. What a lucky coincidence.

My store is a unique tiny 200 square foot hole in the wall that I love. It is full of American Folk Art. I buy hand-made crafts from untrained artisans across the United States. It is a new concept in the city that I created after a trip to Vermont. I thought why not a country store in New York City? I then managed to convince Ira I needed a business and finally he acquiesced. However, what he had feared the most happened. I barely have time to see him. While this suits me just fine it doesn't sit well with him at all.

Jesse is a cross between John Stamos and a young Tony Curtis. He is in his 20s and stands exactly six feet tall. If I were to venture a guess, he weighs about 200 pounds, all muscle. It was as if Michelangelo's David had walked off its base in Florence, Italy and followed me home.

Unlike the perfect statue, Jesse soon tells me he is homeless. He confesses he sleeps in the basement of the hardware store on bags of cement mix. Like moonshine laced with embalming fluid one spark was all it took to blast through the walls I'd built around my heart. He peppered me with sad stories of his poverty-stricken life.

Years from now as I rebuild my life from less than nothing I will go back and think of Chris and Jesse and the hardware store that vanished almost as soon as it appeared.

I toyed with the idea of sleeping with Jesse – a *just for the hell of it fuck* because I wanted a normal guy, not a multi-billionaire married man, and seriously I'm a single woman.

Jessie made me feel something I thought had died within me – a strong sexual stirring from the deepest recesses of my soul. Okay from my loins – but this time from the other side of my fragmented world. The part of me Ira hadn't been able to touch no matter how hard he tried.

He built the bookcase. And afterwards he painted and repainted my living room a pale canary yellow. The first coat was too bright and he softened it for me. Moving day came and he was ever-ready to me with the movers hauling my things from my larger apartment into my smaller one. There was a lot of furniture being crammed into the apartment and it disoriented me because I wasn't sure I'd be able to accommodate everything.

The bookcase was wonderful as it held all my precious books in the same way as my now gone larger apartment.

And then out of nowhere I look around at the mess, the boxes and the overwhelming amount of stuff and start sobbing.

"Why are you crying?" He cradles my face and wipes the tears falling heavy like berries with his hands.

"I don't know why I'm crying... I'm overwhelmed by all of this... The move... Everything... "I start to hiccup and that makes me cry even harder. "I somehow never thought I'd have to move back in here..." I try gasping for air as I blurt out each sentence as I become more and more hysterical.

Jesse pulls me toward him and kisses me. It's startling and impulsively I push him away and because he's not letting me go, I part my lips and his tongue plunges deep into my mouth.

Ira's face pops into my mind and I feel I am betraying him. Even when I am not with him, he manages to walk around with me like second skin so that I am no longer myself, but a combination of the perfect fantasy woman he thinks I am and what he is: an obsessed man.

My splintered soul seems, in this moment inside Jesse's strong arms, to be finally free. As he removes my clothes, he also sheds the shame I've carried for years. I give in to the girl I was before all the bad things happened.

No matter what happens after this, I know I am free.

After that day Jesse spent a lot of time helping me and my staff at the store. He was at the shop when Ira stopped by and it always seemed odd to me that neither one acknowledged the other.

Jesse seemed like a godsend until he wasn't.

A couple of weeks later I open my bank statements and cancelled checks made out to Jesse that I know I haven't written fall out of the thick envelope. My heart shatters like a porcelain vase toppling onto the floor.

I confront him and call the police, who for some odd reason aren't responsive. I can't seem to get help from anyone, not Chris and more surprising, not Ira. It won't be for many years into the future that I will realize it was Ira, all the while, who through Chris and Jessie and a Machiavellian plan gone awry tried to kill me.

～

I tumble into a much-treasured slumber. Just as quickly, I am awakened by loud thumps. Quick heavy steps run across the roof above me. I hear my heart pulsating in my ears as I sit up, hoping that the three deadbolts I've installed on my front door, and the gates I've put on the windows are enough to protect me. For the hundredth time I wonder why Ira took such care to have Dave and his partner install such an intricate alarm system in my store and never did the same for my home.

Someone lands with a thud on my air conditioner. And for a brief moment I think the air conditioner and whoever is on it is going to fall, because the whole wall shakes and the air-conditioner is bent.

Loud guttural screams pour out from the deepest part of my being. I am overcome with fear, and I can't stop screaming because I know I am going to die. In the dark, I reach for the black silk robe I keep at the foot of the bed. I'm halfway into it when I see the fist, then the arm, smashing through my bedroom window. Shards of glass, large and small, spew like popping popcorn into the air. Jesse's contorted face pushes through next and our eyes meet. I am frozen in time and space.

The light from the moon shines from behind him and I can see his face glimmering like a demon from hell, drenched in sweat, soot, and blood. Gone is the face that once reminded me of Michelangelo's David. He has transformed into Jack Nicholson from Stanley Kubrick's *The Shining*.

Twenty-Four

In the wee hours of the morning on June 7, 1991 one of my neighbors, Alexis Ficks Welch, an ex-Rockette working for Ogilvy & Mather's was stabbed to death by a homeless man on her way back to her apartment after walking her two dogs in Central Park. The man identified as Kevin McKiever stabbed her several times, and left her lying on the sidewalk with an 11-inch butcher knife stuck through her kidney and into her spine. She died on the operating room later that morning having lost too much blood for her life to be saved.

Her last words were "I don't want to die."

The story made national headlines because our neighborhood is full of multi-million-dollar condos and depraved crimes like this simply do not happen here.

Everyone in our building went to Alexis's memorial service held at the 100-year-old church across the street. Afterwards, still teary eyed and stunned, we lingered on the sidewalk promising to be extra vigilant so that nothing like this would ever happen to any one of us.

Except that on a Saturday night just before midnight, two weeks later, it happened to me. Despite the blood curdling screams that seeped out of my apartment and into all of my neighbor's homes, no one called the police. Either everyone forgot about our promises or the police ignored their calls too.

Jesse stands on top of the two steps that separate him from where I am in the livingroom, the handle of the large machete-like knife tight in his grip. He has morphed into a demon from hell. His face is shiny with streaks of black tar from the roof, streaks of blood and is flush with sweat.

Time begins to move fast and slow. Like a runaway train speeding down the tracks with no end in sight. One second it is very, very slow; the next very, very fast. I am split between life and death.

His eyes are wild and he fixes them on me.

"I'm here to kill you." He snarls.

Flashes of everything I've ever heard about being in a near death situation run through my mind and I know I am not supposed to try to fight. I sit down on the sofa and look back at him.

"Are you hungry?"

His eyes are wild and he fixes them on me.

He tilts his head slightly.

"You also should take a shower. I'll make you a sandwich."

His wide eyes calm down and he looks confused.

"Okay," he says and places the knife on my table in the hallway.

During the five days he holds me captive in my apartment, he alternates between crazy and sane. There are times when he assaults me and times when he just sits and watches TV. I am a prisoner.

On Thursday I am extra nice to him and tell him I should go to my store or the women who work for me are surely going to send the police. I promise him I won't tell anyone and that when I return, I'll make us something to eat.

I'm wearing a pair of jeans, a top and a pair of sneakers. To my surprise he agrees but warns me that if I don't come back within a half hour he will come after me and kill us all.

I push open the door to my store and am greeted by the sweet aroma of peach potpourri. I race by Jaclyn who is startled to see me and I quickly fill her in. Once inside my tine office upstairs I dial Ira's private line. It doesn't ring like a regular phone, but instead a red light shows up almost like he is Batman or a children's hero.

"Hello."

I blurt it out and end with the words, "I need a bodyguard."

"It's too late for that now."

I'm perplexed as to why it's too late. What am I supposed to do?

"I'll be right over," he says.

And again, I'm confused because I just told him there is a crazed lunatic who is going to kill us all, and all he's ever told me during all these years is how careful he is with his life. That he and his wife often fly separately with only one of them taking the two girls just in case of an accident. That his driver carries a gun in the event of a kidnapping attempt. That he is terrified of his father. Everything he's ever told me is the opposite of what he's doing.

Ten minutes later I hear Ira's heavy footsteps on the steps to my office.

I feel my body shaking and he takes me into his arms.

"You need to leave the city. Take a flight to a place where you don't know anyone. A place you've never been. Go to one city and then buy another ticket and go to a second city. Do not tell anyone where you are going. Don't even tell me."

I nod as I dry my tears.

"Yes, yes, okay. Okay. Okay."

"Take your American Express out of the safe," he instructs.

As soon as I get on my knees and begin turning the knob, Ira exclaims he has to run across the street to Chase Bank, where he's going to get some cash for me.

I'm terrified Jesse will storm into the store and kill him. I don't even count myself in what I see as a massacre. Somehow in my mind's eye I stopped existing after being abducted.

About five minutes later Ira returns and hands me ten crisp $100 bills. He counts each one as he places it into the palm of my hand. I am perplexed by how slow he's moving and the meager amount of money. Nothing makes sense. It's always he who has been afraid of being kidnapped or murdered. But, somehow he's here and he doesn't seem concerned or scared. For a billionaire, $1,000 to keep me safe, seems to me unusually bizarre. Time is running out and so I opt to say nothing.

"Pay for the airplane tickets with cash," he advises. "Use your credit card for the hotel. Go to the nearest airport." Then, he pulls me close to him and kisses me. A full wet tongue kiss while I feel dead inside. In years to come I will remember this obscene gesture as his kiss of death. I silently try to understand how far or safe I can be on a $1,000.

I run out into the street, hail a cab, and with his words ringing in my ears "Go to the nearest airport" I almost say La Guardia which is closer, but instead I tell the driver to take me to JFK.

I pluck down six one hundred-dollar bills to pay for my one-way ticket to Los Angeles which leaves in about one hour. I stop at a pay phone and call Steve, one of my best friends, in Los Angeles.

"I'm getting on a plane and am on my way. Can you pick me up at 5:30?"

"I'll be there."

After rattling off the terrifying details of my ordeal and telling him I'm terrified of being alone he invites me to stay at his apartment. I'm grateful for his generosity and agree. Going to a city I've never been to, as Ira wanted me to do, made no sense to me.

On Sunday I phone my store manager. Connie is a responsible 23-year old who worked at the bakery across the street from my shop before working for me.

"I stopped by your apartment. It's gone. Everything you own is destroyed," she starts crying uncontrollably. "I'm so sorry, it's gone. "It's gone, it's gone. Everything you have is gone?"

"What do you mean?"

"It's all trashed. There is nothing left of your things. Not the furniture, not your clothes, nothing."

I felt numb. It really did not register. All I knew was that I panned to do whatever was required to put Jesse behind bars.

I immediately call the police in New York and tell them what Connie has just explained but they claim that unless I'm inside the apartment they can't do anything. I place the cost of a one-way ticket to New York on my American Express, hire a body guard and fly back to New York less than one week after I escaped with my life. For reasons I do not know Ira will not help me hire a bodyguard, nor will he pay for one.

Roscoe looks like he belongs in the corporate world instead of a gun-toting private eye turned body guard when the need arose. He retired from the police force in New York over one decade ago. He rose through the ranks from patrol officer up to detective. In a place like New York this requires quick thinking and street smarts.

He meets me at the airport and I spot him holding a cardboard sign with my name on it.

"I'd like to see my apartment before dropping my bags off at the hotel," I tell him as we climb into his black sedan in the parking lot of the airport.

"Sure thing," we're soon on the Long Island Expressway where I spot the familiar Twin Towers with the smaller Empire State building as we approach the city.

The Empire State building always reminds me of King Kong in the 1933 version with the gigantic gorilla with human-like qualities. Instead of killing the sacrificial victim who has been offered to him by the natives of Skull Island, King Kong carries her off in the palm of his hand. The art deco 102-story Empire State Building was only two years old when we saw Kong climb up the building. The movie was made by RKO which at the time was owned by Joseph P. Kennedy – who later sold it to Meshulam Riklis.

Walking into my apartment was like falling into hell. The floor is covered three inches deep with feathers and powder. It takes me a few minutes to realize the feathers are from my two matching sofas that have been slashed open and the mattress on my bed. All my clothes have been piled up into the bathtub where they are soaked in paint, feathers and blood. The walls have scrawled hand-written messages written in lipstick and blood.

While I do not make the connection to Charles Manson while standing in the middle of my destroyed home with blood splattered everywhere I will never be able to think about it again without comparing it to Sharon Tate's murder and the word "PIG" scrawled on the front door with her blood.

However, someone has already painted over many of the words scribbled on the wall and I don't know that the crime scene had already been tainted.

"Are you okay?" Roscoe asks gently touching my elbow as I make my way into the apartment.

"I'm fine," I reply with sincerity because I seriously can't feel anything. I'm numb. It's a place where I will stay for the next year of my life.

I climb over the remnants of my furniture that look like they've been in a hurricane, scattered here and there, to look out the window. I'm not searching for anything special but as I tilt my head back and glance up at the roof of the building across the street. I gasp. I see Jesse's dark head of hair sitting on the ledge. He's staring back at me.

"Roscoe, come look, quickly!" I point up and Jesse darts out of our line of vision.

"I saw him, don't worry. I've got a gun and I have no problem using it if I have to. Come on," he says, "let's go to the police station."

The police respond to Roscoe because he identifies himself as a former detective. To this point despite the many times I contacted them, they have for reasons unknown to me refused to help. One of the police officers even told me that unless I was dead there was nothing they could do.

This time, in less than one hour, an assortment of twenty police officers and detectives escorted Roscoe and myself back to my little apartment that was now a garbage dump.

Everything was destroyed. All my furniture, all my clothes, all my pictures. My entire life up until this time vanished.

As I stand in my apartment with Roscoe and over 20 seasoned detectives squeezed in around me, I overhear one of them whisper, "Geez, she would have been found here in pieces."

TWENTY-FIVE

It is a cloudy September afternoon and my second time in New York since I helped the police capture Jessie. Roscoe picked me up at the airport and once again took precaution driving into Manhattan making sure no one was following the car.

I am going to testify in front of the grand jury in the morning. Using an alias, I check into a privately owned hotel, and instruct the desk clerk I am not to be disturbed: no phone calls, no maid service, nothing.

Only two people know where I am: Roscoe and Ira Riklis.

As instructed, I call Ira after unpacking, and he insists on seeing me. I'm walking distance from both his apartment and his office. Since I can't afford a suite and Ira hasn't offered to pay for my bodyguard, I'm in one of the smaller rooms. I give him the room number as I have done many times before so that he doesn't have to stop at the desk. After he knocks on the door, I ask Roscoe to wait outside.

Ira walks in and immediately embraces me. He tries to tongue kiss me. I can't. I just can't and sincerely cannot believe he thinks it's life as usual. I push him away and he plops down on the foot of the bed. Exasperated I sit next to him.

"You're so brave," he says solemnly as placing his hand on my thigh. His eyes always heavy with dark circles look almost ashen grey against his puffy face.

Instead of getting solace or feeling emboldened by his apparent faith in me—his words sound shallow. Why didn't he contact the police? Certainly he had access to a world of people who could have helped me. But he did nothing and he's here and wants to make out like nothing happened and I just can't.

I even want to cry. This whole thing is just so weird. But I don't want to extend his visit, nor do I need for him to comfort me. I spot the letter size manila envelope he's cradling in his left hand.

"You've always been braver than I will ever be," he says and then reaches inside the envelope, "I brought this for you."

I don't know what to expect but when I see him pulling out pages of a recent *New York Magazine* article with a front page photo of my neighbor Alexis Fichs Welsh who was just murdered I want to scream.

The title is *Dance of Death*.

"It's about your neighbor, I thought you'd want to read it." He hands me the offending sheets of paper and I place them on the bed. I try not looking at them. I need him to go away. Feeling lightheaded I stand up and walk the four steps to the oblong window. He joins me wrapping his arm around my waist and continues talking. I zone out. I can't listen to him anymore. I'm completely freaked out. I don't understand why he would cut out this article at this time. Alexis was murdered two weeks before my attack. None of his actions make any sense to me.

And since I am not responding to his romantic overtures he decides it's time to leave. Relieved I shut the door behind him and jam the offending images of the now dead Alexis into the bottom of my overnight bag.

Roscoe and I begin to discuss what I should expect the following morning when someone knocks heavily at the door.

Two men stand on the other side. One introduces himself as the manager of the hotel who I recognize having seen him behind the check-in desk. He points to the man next to him and tells us he is the owner.

"Come in," I say.

"We're sorry to bother you but it is our understanding you told us you were not expecting any calls," the hotel manager asks.

Both men have frowns on their faces.

"I'm not."

"That's odd because about one hundred phone calls have come into the hotel since you checked in earlier," the hotel manager says his arms moving in an exaggerated motion as if to echo his words.

"What?" I exclaim, "No, you must be mistaken. No one knows I'm here."

"Someone knows you're here," the owner says, "and we're concerned. Is there something you want to share with us?"

The stack of photos taken of my apartment are in my handbag. I grab it and pull them out.

"I am the victim of a crime," I tell them as I hand them the pictures so they can see for themselves.

"Yes," adds Roscoe, "Kirby is going to be testifying in front of a grand jury in the morning. However, no one knows she's here except for myself and her boyfriend who just left."

The two men are shaking their heads and passing the photos back and forth among them. The manager hands them back to me.

"We cannot have a dead girl found in our hotel and I am afraid if you stay that is what will happen."

The owner looks at me with an intense sadness in his eyes. "We are sorry, you will have to pack your bags and leave. It is not a chance we want to take with your life."

TWENTY-SIX

Once we're back in Roscoe's car he tells me to buckle up.

"I'm going to be running red lights and driving erratically," he explains. "Someone is following you and I'm going to lose the son-of-a-bitch."

My heart's pounding really fast against my chest as the car takes off. It feels surreal—like I'm in a movie with the car swirling and cutting off other cars as it races through the streets of New York. True to his word

Roscoe drives past red lights ignoring the honking horns and screeching tires as cars swerve to avoid us. He finally comes to a stop at a hotel where only cheap tourists stay.

"No one will find you here. You'll be safe. Right after you testify in the morning, I'll get you back on a plane to Los Angeles. You're not safe here."

I am numb and follow instructions at this point like the tiny ballerina inside a vintage music box. Round and round to the music that simply repeats and repeats without getting anywhere.

I can't sleep, but begin to get dressed for court at 6am. One hour later, I take the elevator down to the lobby where Roscoe is waiting.

He takes my arm and ushers me out onto the busy street.

"I want you to know I am going to be holding on to my gun which is under my arm when we walk from the car to the courthouse. If anyone tries anything, Kirby, I'm going to pop them."

Everything happened very fast and very slow. My being sworn in. My answering the questions. My looking at the jurors—one of whom I recognized as a woman I sublet an apartment from ages ago. I wanted to see the reaction of the people to the photos when they were passed around. Each one of them looked at the photo, handed it to the next person and then looked at me with pity. It was embarrassing. I didn't want to be pitied. The assistant district attorney, John, never brought up the rape or anything about the break-in. No one, especially not Ira, gave me any advice. I knew nothing about the law or how it worked. I just floated along believing the "system" somehow was going to protect me. I was wrong. The system is not meant to protect me—it is there to protect the masters of the universe. However, it would take a long time for me to have the ability to wrap my mind around this harsh reality.

And then it was over. The assistant district attorney told me in the corridor of the courthouse to let Jesse plea because at least he would do a minimum of five years in jail. He'd been in jail since the day I was able to catch him which was a couple of months ago. I agreed because no one explained the legal process to me and it never occurred to me to speak to an attorney. In the end, to my horror, Jesse served a mere four months and was released. Decades later, I would discover Jesse was with a police department in upstate New York. I found one mention of him online as being a detective. When I began to work on this book I tried to find it again—it was gone.

My friends in Los Angeles repeatedly insisted I had been "set up" by Ira and I, in turn, replied, "No, he helped me escape." It took a long time before I saw what my friends saw.

Twenty-Seven

1993

Ira and I have the same travel agent. His name is Paul. I met Paul years ago before Ira marched back into my life on a flight to Miami to meet my then boyfriend for the weekend.

It was in the mid-1980s.

I took the window seat and Paul sat next to me in the aisle. He was very chatty and even before the flight took off, he told me his name, explained that he was a travel agent as such he could save me a lot of money. Paul bore a strong resemblance to a shorter Jay Leno. With the same full hair and wisps of gray on his temples.

"Meet your new client," I replied enthusiastically shaking his hand slipping his card into my purse. We chatted for the duration of the three-hour flight, and as the plane landed, I remember he gave me a bizarre set of instructions.

"I don't want your boyfriend to get jealous so I won't walk out of the plane with you. You go first."

"Ok," I uttered feeling somewhat uneasy but I didn't want to make a big deal out of it. A couple of minutes later as I was hugging and kissing my boyfriend I saw Paul walk past us. His eyes locked into mine and I noticed the way he looked at my boyfriend. From head to toe which is odd for one straight man to look at another straight man. I felt a tinge of guilt in the pit of my stomach and quickly decided I was over-reacting. I slipped my arm through my boyfriend's arm and we made our way out of the airport and back to an apartment he kept in Miami.

Two years later after Paul and I had gone to the movies, after he'd taken me to Cirque du Soleil, after I spent hours at his office sharing the most intimate

245

details of my life, after he became my friend, he told me he was also Ira's travel agent. At the time it seemed coincidental. I would only see the Machiavellian scheme many years into the future and even when I realized it, I would try to imagine it differently. Such a betrayal by a person who managed to slip into my life so easily was crushing. It would forever alter the way I perceived any new person who appeared in my life. The first time I ever heard anything similar with when Rose McGowen's story about being befriended by a former Mossad agent working for a firm named Black Cube and written by Ronan Farrow showed up in *The New Yorker* in 2017.

On the day I decided it was time to say goodbye to Ira it was Paul's New York phone number I dialed. For two reasons. First, I wanted him to book my trip from Los Angeles to New York and back. Second, I needed for him to confirm Ira was in the city and not elsewhere.

"Hi gorgeous, it's nice to hear from you!" He chirps cheerily.

"Thanks, Paul, I need a ticket to the city. Do you have a couple of minutes?"

"Sure, what are your dates?"

"I'm going to say goodbye to Ira and I need to get my cue from you. He goes to North Carolina so often I don't want to sit around waiting. I wanted to see what you would suggest."

"Wow. That's a big step. You, uhm, are you sure you want to do that?" He sounds stunned. I can tell because he's enunciating every word.

"Yes, I am sure. I am more sure than I have been about anything else."

"Ok, then. I don't have him traveling anywhere so yes he will be at his office when you arrive on Monday."

~

Although Ira's hold on me extends far beyond 3,000 miles that separate us, I manage to have enough time alone to realign myself with the child of great determination I once knew, and realize that if I continue along this path, my entire life will be misspent. I have to do something, and I know I have to do it soon. During the times Ira summons me to New York and puts me up at the St. Regis Hotel, or stops through Los Angeles during his business trips, I find myself looking at him differently. This man who years into the future I'd realize had told me nothing but lies; also kept me in self-doubt, insecurity and fear. Not surprising, his control was similar to my mother's.

In the fall of 1993, I finally do two things that took me a lifetime to do -- I have a heart to heart with my mother, and I leave Ira. My mother refuses to acknowledge she's done anything wrong. I know better and realize that if only one of us is going to change, it's going to have to be me.

And when I told Ira it was over, walking away from his safety net, I realize he hadn't given me one at all. At the final moment he reneged on the money he'd promised to give me at the end of our relationship. "Millions," he'd promised so many times. "Don't worry, you'll never have to work again, when the day comes, I will take care of you."

When he callously reneged it didn't matter anymore. I was free. I boarded the plane back to Los Angeles with less than $100 to my name. I felt light and free and even happy. Happy was something I hadn't felt in a very long time. I knew I'd have to do a lot to piece together my life but it didn't feel daunting or so far away anymore.

In a rare moment of clarity, I realized that not unlike Dorothy in Oz, the safety net I'd come to depend on Ira for, had been with me all along. In fact, it belonged to the girl I had once been. So, I did what any other woman would do: I scooped it up, wrapped it around myself and have carried it with me all these many years since.

～

If this were a fairytale my memoir would end here. However, it's real life. My life. That day was simply the beginning of a lifetime of terror. There have been more attempts on my life. My family has been unsafe. Anytime I create an online presence it is constantly tampered with. When I try to get a business off the ground, it is destroyed. This becomes a vicious cycle.

Someone or something lurks in my shadow. The world changes like the tides of the ocean. Had I never struggled, it would have been impossible for me to adapt, fight back and stay alive.

In time, I will learn the shadows are part of a larger octopus—one I never knew existed. It will take years before the invisible becomes clearly defined—at least to me.

Epilogue

On a seemingly normal day I opened the front door of my apartment to go run a couple of errands. Lying on my doorstep was a book that wasn't gift-wrapped. It was just sitting on the floor pushed against my door and had a note written on a pink sheet of paper.

"Another night, another dream, but always you." The word *'always'* is underlined.

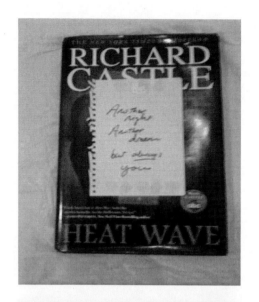

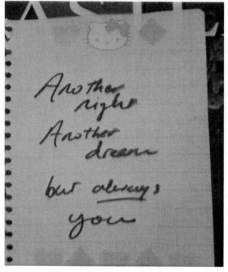

Being in a rush, as I usually am, I tossed the benign looking book onto the small kitchen cart where it landed on top of about a dozen pieces of unopened mail.

A few hours later while on the phone with a friend I asked him if he had left the book on my doorstep. "No, of course not. I'm in New Jersey. Maybe one of your neighbors left it."

I then quizzed some of my neighbors and a new man I'd been dating for a couple of months.

No one I knew left the book on my doorstep.

Perplexed, I decided to examine it more carefully.

The first thing that caught my attention were some of the words on the book jacket:

"A New York real estate tycoon plunges to his death on a Manhattan sidewalk. A trophy wife with a past survives a narrow escape from a brazen attack. Mobsters and moguls with no shortage of reasons to kill trot out their alibis…"

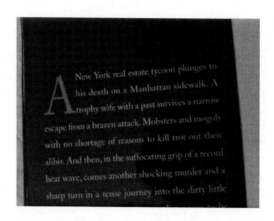

A New York real estate tycoon plunges to his death on a Manhattan sidewalk. A trophy wife with a past survives a narrow escape from a brazen attack. Mobsters and moguls with no shortage of reasons to kill trot out their alibis. And then, in the suffocating grip of a record heat wave, comes another shocking murder and a sharp turn in a tense journey into the dirty little

The words "real estate," "trophy wife with a past," "survives a narrow escape from a brazen attack," "mobsters and moguls," made my heart skip a beat and my pulse race. I'm in the real estate business. I was someone's trophy wife. I survived a narrow escape from a brazen attack. The coincidences were too many for this to be a regular book.

It had to be a message. One of many left for me throughout the years. I was determined to find out what it meant.

I then noticed the scent on the Hello Kitty note paper that had the writing. It smelled just like Chloe. One of the two perfumes Ira offered me years ago when his father purchased Elizabeth Arden.

The words went round and round in my mind because they seemed vaguely familiar. I simply didn't know what they meant.

"Another day
Another dream
But always you."

I put them into a google search. And, what I discovered frightened me.

The words are from the song *Another Night* by Real McCoy.

Every morning right before stepping onto my treadmill, I play that song. It's part of a 1990s mix I work out to.

I realize that whoever left the book with the note by my door wanted me to know they were close enough to hear me. Which meant someone was standing just outside my door more than once to know it was part of my morning routine.

Whenever I have been scared, it has pushed me to go further. It doesn't make me give up. Instead it propels me to try to find answers.

The pink Hello Kitty notepaper stood out as another oddity.

Not being of the Hello Kitty generation, I googled "Hello Kitty."

Two things alarmed me:

First, Hello Kitty has no mouth. Therefore she cannot speak. I have been silenced for so very long and this chilled my soul.

The second thing was even more terrifying. It was a reference to the "Hello Kitty murder".

The Hello Kitty murder happened in 1999 in Hong Kong. A woman was kidnapped and tortured in her apartment for one long excruciating month. After her abductors killed her she was decapitated and her head was stuffed into a Hello Kitty doll.

Having been "kidnapped and held in her apartment" had also happened to me. There were simply too many coincidences with everything about the book jacket cover and the written note with the horrible facts of the gruesome Hello Kitty murder.

I called my boyfriend and asked him to come over to my apartment. I wanted to make sure that the perfume I smelled on the note was indeed Chloe and so I asked him to stop by Chloe on Fifth Avenue and pick up a sample of their classic perfume.

When he arrived in my apartment about two hours later and after I filled him in on the book and all the things I'd discovered, he looked even more horrified than I felt. Even this was familiar to me. A terrified boyfriend. Someone who had gotten close enough to begin a life with who, for one reason or another, became afraid of being in my life.

He handed me the bag with the Chloe sample.

"They told me they don't have the original anymore," he said, "but they explained this is not that different."

We both smelled the book and the perfume.

It was a match.

"How did you know it was Chloe?" he asked, his brow creasing with concern and his blue eyes suddenly still.

"Because all of this," I explained as I held the book in my hands. I pause and then begin again, "All of this has to come from the Riklis people. When they owned Elizabeth Arden he gave me a lifetime supply of one of the two fragrances."

"You mean Chloe?"

"No, his wife preferred Chloe. I liked the other one Narcisse Noir de Caron."

"Why do you think they left this here?"

"To keep me perpetually afraid."

~

In the sequel *Cinderella Doesn't Live Here Anymore* I share the series of strange events that follow me throughout the years. Some connected to intelligence agencies; but all meant to make me disappear—physically, morally and in every way imaginable. In order to stay alive, I teach myself how to connect the myriad of clues that ultimately led me to the Jeffrey Epstein case.

About The Author

Kirby Sommers is the author of over a dozen books. She is an investigative journalist an advocate for human rights. She writes the weekly *Epstein Project* newsletter and hosts the *Epstein Project* podcast. Her books include *The Billionaire's Woman: A Memoir, Jeffrey Epstein Predator Spy*, *Jeffrey Epstein, Revealed* (co-authored with Bob Fitrakis), *Bonnie's Clyde: The True Story of Jeffrey Epstein and Ghislaine Maxwell*, and several others. For a full list, please visit her website: kirbysommers.com.

Kirby's ability to transcend and help others was featured in a Tedx Talk presented by Justin Constantine titled, *You Are Stronger Than You Think You Are*.

Ms. Sommers lives in New York and is currently writing a sequel to her memoir *The Billionaire's Woman* named *Cinderella Doesn't Live Here Anymore*; as well the sequel to *Ghislaine Maxwell: An Unauthorized Biography* titled *Ghislaine Maxwell, Blackmail*. Both books are scheduled for release in the Spring of 2023.

Kirby Sommers

The Billionaire's Woman:
Memoir of a Sex Slave

Website: kirbysommers.com

To join mailing list:
https://kirbysommers.com/mailing-list

Twitter: @kirbysommers

Kirby Sommers

For every survivor,
everywhere

Kirby Sommers

•

Made in United States
North Haven, CT
12 February 2025

65785179R00159